W9-BBB-224

CRIMES AGAINST AMERICA

CRIMES AGAINST AMERICA

THE LEFT'S TAKEDOWN OF OUR REPUBLIC

JUDGE JEANINE PIRRO

This book is dedicated to my grandson, Cameron. My hope is that he will grow up brave and free, in the nation with that shining city on the hill, that we can all hopefully still recognize and celebrate as the greatest country on this earth.

At what point shall we expect the approach of danger? By what means shall we fortify against it?—Shall we expect some transatlantic military giant, to step the Ocean, and crush us at a blow? Never!—All the armies of Europe, Asia and Africa combined, with all the treasure of the earth (our own excepted) in their military chest; with a Buonaparte for a commander, could not by force, take a drink from the Ohio, or make a track on the Blue Ridge, in a trial of a thousand years.

At what point then is the approach of danger to be expected? I answer, if it ever reach us, it must spring up amongst us. It cannot come from abroad. If destruction be our lot, we must ourselves be its author and finisher. As a nation of freemen, we must live through all time, or die by suicide.

—Abraham Lincoln, Speech to the Young Men's Lyceum
of Springfield, 1838

CONTENTS

CRIMES
AGAINST
AMERICA

THE INDICTMENT

The America I was born into was indisputably the greatest nation that has ever existed in the history of the world.

It was the richest country in the world. It had the most powerful military in the world. It was the world's chief scientific innovator. Its people were the healthiest, the most educated, and the most productive. Its cities were world-class hubs not just for industry, but for art and culture. American scientists and engineers put a man on the moon.

It was a great country. And now, it exists only in my memories.

The America of my childhood, the America so much of the world dreamed of throughout the twentieth century, is no more. Her national unity has been compromised. Her wealth has been plundered. She has suffered assaults to her bedrock principles, from freedom of speech and religion to capitalist, market-based economics. Her world-class schools now spread indoctrination, and the National Assessment for Education Progress reports that many high school seniors can't read or do math.

And at the top of it all—a visceral symbol of national decline if there ever was one—is President Joe Biden. Never in the history of this nation has one president done so much damage in so little

3

time as Biden. At times, his actions have been so destructive, they are indistinguishable from what a foreign saboteur would do. Biden has thrown away America's energy independence, exposing us to our enemies. He has taken away the incentive to work in favor of an ever-more-socialist system where rewards are doled out based on skin and sex and orientation rather than ability. He has treated our border not as something to protect but as an obstacle to be removed. He has shattered our national unity with dark speeches declaring half the country fundamentally irredeemable because of how it votes and its belief in the greatness of America.

To put Biden in power, an unprecedented assault on the freedom of speech was needed in order to conceal the actions of perhaps the blackest sheep in the history of presidential family members.

America used to be a cut above. Our politicians could make mistakes, but we could at least take for granted they would be impressive men and women (or at least be awake most of the time). Corruption happened, but also inspired outrage and reform.

Now, America is becoming something we've never been before: we are becoming *unexceptional*. We are becoming just another country that "elects" puppet leaders who enrich their families and rubber-stamp the agenda of their handlers. Our exceptional rights— our right to bear arms, our exceptionally far-reaching freedom of speech—are giving way to easily-curtailed "rights" (a.k.a. restrictions) that pass for freedom in the rest of the world. The Left's so-called "progressiveness" in America is merely rolling backward to the dark ages of Marxism and socialism.

The America of today does not simply reflect the natural evolution of a changing society. The America of today reflects the damage done by an intentional takedown of the greatest nation on earth. In most cases, by those offended by her very excellence. What has happened to us isn't natural decay. It's not an accident or a fluke. It's the product of a series of crimes—Crimes against America.

Over the following eleven chapters, I will lay out eleven crimes against America. They are not conventional crimes, like those I once prosecuted as a district attorney, or those which have become increasingly common on our city streets. But they are moral crimes, atrocities against our nation and offenses against our children, who will inherit a nation far worse off than the one they deserve. Some of these crimes are dark humor, like our reminder that each day of President Biden is another day of witnessing elder abuse. But most crimes are not—they are of great concern to the future of our nation. There's the Left's gaslighting of America into abandoning the fossil fuels that have made us prosperous. There are the lies of the Black Lives Matter movement that have disempowered our police and sowed chaos in our city streets. Above all, the meltdown at the border is so serious and so sustained that it calls into question whether America remains a country at all—after all, isn't a country supposed to have a border?

The chief perpetrator of these crimes, in theory, is Joe Biden, but you're kidding yourself if you think he's the mastermind here. He is not. As I will explain in the chapters that follow, Biden is merely the Trojan Horse—a convenient, fake moderate. An empty suit and the Left's leftover from a better era, used to infiltrate the White House so the people with actual socialist ideas can get to work taking down America.

What follows is a true crime story: I won't just show you *who* is committing the crimes, but *how* they pulled off their dastardly schemes. These offenses are founded on something quite simple and straightforward—facts that are not themselves mysterious at all. The mystery comes in how the crime is covered up. The trick has been to distract you—with noise, with yelping about "Russia!" and "Racism!" so you don't see what is going on in plain sight, in Washington, or at the border, or in your own schools and cities.

I have done my best in this book to walk you through the Left's strategies in pulling off their Crimes against America. The question is: Have they succeeded?

A Breach of Sovereignty

Most Americans sense that something has changed in the country we live in. Something has shifted. "America" doesn't represent what it once did. It doesn't reflect the values and strength and vitality that the name once carried.

But this actually undersells what has happened. It's more than simple generational evolution. It's that the America of even ten years ago no longer exists. Something in America has changed. It's not normal change, the inevitable evolving and shifting that comes with the passage of time. In fact, "change" isn't the right word for it. America has become warped. The America envisioned by our Founding Fathers, the America preserved and built up by the generations who came after them, is no more. America, after all, was a country. Countries have a territory, borders, and a representative accountable government. More and more every day, it's clear that America actually has none of these things. The country has been forcibly mutated into little more than a globalist landing pad with benefits.

This warped, liberal version of America rejects everything that came before it. It rejects the Declaration of Independence that birthed our country. It rejects the Constitution that gave it its shape. It rejects the great heroes, from Washington to Jefferson to Lincoln, who gave it life. It rejects America's history, and the people who lived it, as just a parade of racism and bigotry that should be consigned to the ash heap of history, along with the statues representing them.

With the Left's rejection of the old America has come a rejection of the values that made it great: ordered liberty, freedom of speech, the presumption of innocence, the right to bear arms.

So if the Left rejects the values of old America, the founding documents of old America, the history of old America, and indeed the *descendants* of old America, what remains? Certainly nothing that my father or grandfather would recognize as the country they fought for.

That, in turn, is the root of the vanished sovereignty we see at the American border. If America and its people hold no value, then why should either of them be preserved? The answer, for more and more of President Biden's ilk, is: they shouldn't be.

Just a few years ago, it was politically incorrect—professionally dangerous, in fact—to call the deluge of "migrants" at our southern border what it actually is. Just mentioning the word "invasion" would get you called a racist. Mentioning the end goal—bringing in more Democrat-leaning-voters—will still prompt calls for a person to be literally canceled.

But the fun thing about words is that they matter. As the Soviets learned, no power on earth can forever suppress a statement that is indisputably true. And when it comes to our border, the true statement is this: America is being invaded, without a shot being fired, with the active connivance of our ruling class.

The situation on our southern border is so unbelievable, so unprecedented, that it's difficult to even think about. In the 2021 fiscal year, Customs and Border Protection encountered 1.72 million people along the border, an all-time record. Then, in 2022, they broke that record by *more than a million*, reaching 2.76 million encounters.[1] That's more than five people crossing the border illegally every minute for an entire year. And that word, "encounters," alludes to a deeper truth: Those 2.76 million are just the arrivals we know about. No doubt, tens or hundreds of thousands more are arriving sight unseen. In January of 2023 alone Border Patrol estimated 100,000 getaways, or non-encounters. In 2018, the human smuggling business at the border was a $500 million business. Today, it has grown to more than $13 billion.[2]

With a human torrent on that scale, the word "border" ceases to hold any meaning. The American flag has been pulled down, and a white flag of surrender flies at full mast.

While these arrivals are crossing the Mexican border, the days where Mexico itself supplies the overwhelming majority of illegal migrants are long-gone. Thanks to the internet, the non-existence of America's border has become public knowledge worldwide. Illegal migrants fly in literally from around the world to take their turn fording the Rio Grande and declaring themselves in search of "asylum." Many arrive with no identification. Border Patrol sources say those with identification are told to ditch them before they cross over into this country. We have no way of telling who they are, or if a single thing they say is true. We don't know if they are terrorists, criminals, addicts, or insane. And every day, more of them come, and we graciously let them into America, without resistance.

No nation in history has ever had such a huge number of people arrive in such a short span. At the absolute peak of its activity,

Ellis Island admitted barely 1 million people—and those people all arrived legally, and were not only proud to be in America, they swore allegiance to this country. Many of them kissing the ground when they arrived.

I know that America is not a country hostile to immigrants. But it is also clear that things are not as they were. The 2.7 million people blitzing the U.S.-Mexico border are not like the Ellis Island arrivals of a century ago. And in the age of smartphones, social media, and the internet, America's power to absorb and assimilate new arrivals is not what it once was. When my grandparents came here, they were cut off from their old country and old ways entirely, and had to accept the ways of the new country they had come to. Today, an illegal immigrant is just one Skype call away from every relative they've left behind . . . although when they tell them how easy it was to get to America, odds are those relatives won't be "left behind" for very long.

This invasion is not covert. It is not hidden from sight. It is open, continuous, and notorious. At this point, it has become so flagrant that television (well, not left-wing television) has built an entire cottage industry out of tracking "migrant caravans" as they pass from Guatemala, all the way up through Mexico, and into the U.S.

How many is enough? How much can we afford? How much can our overburdened schools and hospitals and shelters handle? Right now in this country, there is a shortage of housing. Is it any wonder why? When will it end? *Will* it end? What in the world is Joe Biden doing? More importantly, why is he doing it? Why is he allowing this to happen—and "allow" is the correct word in this case, because nobody who really wanted to end this crisis would put Kamala Harris in charge of fixing it.

For President Biden, the border meltdown is a low priority, because Americans seem to be a low priority. He is fine with an America-last agenda. It took three centuries for America to grow from a tiny, fringe colony of England to the richest nation in history. Now, Biden seems determined to destroy that prosperity, burning it all up in a single massive conflagration.

I myself am the granddaughter of immigrants, who came here from far-off Lebanon. My grandfather was so proud of his newly-adopted country that he volunteered for the Navy during World War II. He flew the American flag in front of his home every day. My grandfather might have had a foreign origin, but he was a proud American to his core. My American-born father did the same.

The most radical factions of the progressive Left, once regarded as a handful of freaks, have seized de facto control of the United States government. They disguise this accomplishment by trotting out a "moderate" in Joe Biden. Biden is presented as a centrist, but we only have to ask ourselves: On what issues is Biden to the right of Barack Obama when he was president? The answer, of course, is "essentially none of them." When Barack Obama ran for president in 2008, he promised to protect the border. He even opposed gay marriage! None of that will fly in the Biden White House. But it's more than just the signature issues. The Biden administration is the administration of Rachel Levine, and Sam Brinton, and "non-binary" TikTok influencers holding White House internships. The administration speaks a lingo—"microaggressions," "systemic racism," "LGBTQIA"—that only existed in college classrooms fifteen years ago.

Yet while embracing radicalism, the Biden administration accuses its opponents of being a threat to the republic. In August 2022, during a speech at a fundraising event in Maryland, Joe Biden said that "extreme" Republicans were practicing something "like semi-fascism."³ In a September speech at Independence Hall, standing in front of a blood-red background, Biden denounced 75 million Trump voters, the "MAGA Republicans," as an existential threat to freedom and democracy!⁴ According to the President of the United States, half the electorate is an existential threat to the country, but a literal invading torrent at the border is not.

But in some ways, Biden's assumption makes sense. For progressives, America is not a country as traditionally understood—a people possessing their own history and government and culture and way of life. America is just the realm of the Democratic Party, subject to their power and control. Viewed that way, then MAGA Republicans really are an existential threat—they get in the way. And that horde of illegal immigrants? They aren't a threat in the slightest. In fact, they're part of the plan.

COUNT TWO

Perjury

I t's no secret that the American political system is no longer the
level playing field it once was. The mainstream press has always
leaned a little left, and conservatives haven't always gotten the best
coverage in our nation's newspapers. Those of us who favor stability
and trust in our institutions have always had to fight a little harder
for attention than those who believe we should just burn everything
down and start over.

Conservatives, however, no longer have to contend only with
their opponents on the Left. Instead, we are forced to battle leftist
ideologues—who have been coming together slowly over the past
few election cycles, who reached their final, most terrifying form
during the presidential election of 2020.

The notion that someone in the government—or someone
acting on behalf of the government—would attempt to censor
conservative views in secret never seemed all that far-fetched. We
remembered, after all, that just before President Barack Obama ran
for reelection, several conservative groups were shaken down by the

Internal Revenue Service, seemingly for random routine tax audits and other procedures. But after a little digging, it was revealed that these groups had been on a list of "undesirables" all along, singled out for censorship and dirty tricks by the regime. Initially the assumption was that young ideologues who believed it their mission to squash opposing views were at play—that they were putting their communist imprimatur on our tax code. You remember, "I plead the fifth," Lois Lerner.

After the targeting of conservatives by the Obama administration was found out, they didn't stop censoring conservatives. Instead, they got more creative about it, delegating the work to social media companies, who felt no obligation to come clean about their nefarious activities to the public. When asked about it, they could lie with absolutely no repercussions.

These are crimes against America, and if they are not punished, this nation will quickly lose not only its moral compass and sovereignty, but its long-cherished place as the greatest nation on earth.

These people have been telling us for years that the United States is an evil, backward country that stands for nothing more than racism and oppression, and they will not stop until they're right.

So what happened? Why does it seem that a small band of radical leftists who once held no power continue to exert such an outsize influence on American politics? How is it that a few freaks and misfits, once confined to the outer edges of the Democrat Party and the homepage of Twitter, have control of not only the White House, but defied history by surviving historically anti-incumbent massacre of the midterm elections almost unscathed?

Is the system *really* that broken? It is when the intelligence community positions itself with the Left.

The first of this monster's many heads is the dark, incestuous Intelligence Community. This is where Swamp Creatures such as the FBI's pious self-righteous Cardinal James Comey, his apostle Andrew McCabe, the CIA's John Brennan, and the DNI head James Clapper worked to cook up lies about Russia Collusion and secret dossiers for the entirety of the Trump presidency.

It's where our once-respected supposedly non-partisan agents of the government created fake documents to obtain a court's permission necessary to spy on a politician they didn't like, then denied and lied for years about having done so. This is the group of partisan hacks who told us in the lead-up to the 2020 election that the soon-to-be-infamous Hunter Biden laptop contained "all the earmarks of Russian disinformation," and that news organizations were right to suppress that information in what became of prior restraint.[1] A historic and unparalleled example of prior restraint and censorship of the press.

The Radical Left is closer than ever to its goal of tearing down the United States of America. They have come so close to achieving this goal by breaking every established norm of American politics and by corrupting our major institutions, from Fortune 500 to universities, media institutions, and even hospitals. They have torn down our monuments, denied basic biology, and attempted to indoctrinate our children at a level not seen since the days of Karl Marx. They deny their wrongdoing by lying to us, and they govern by lying to us.

Beside the intelligence community, the mainstream media, a group of people so disconnected from regular, working Americans that I'm surprised they don't just climb into a rocket and blast off to Mars to report back from another stratosphere. Rather than reporting fairly and accurately about both of this country's political parties, the major networks and newspapers of this country have all thrown their support behind the Democrats and their leftist Marxist agenda.

They used to be quiet about this. They used to make attempts to hide it. When you confronted them, they used to claim that they were fair, unbiased, and balanced in their coverage.

That is no longer the case.

By now, it's hardly even worth pointing out that sometime around 2015—for whatever reason—mainstream news networks began to see themselves not as unbiased purveyors of information, but as noble social justice warriors fighting racism, sexism, and fascism with their stories. Rather than trained journalists who wanted to report the truth no matter what the political consequences, the employees of these newsrooms were younger, crazier, and more ideologically focused than ever before. When the facts led them to places that flat-out contradicted their reporting or that made them uncomfortable, they simply ignored those facts.

But first, let's take a quick trip back in time, shall we? Back to the moments before Biden and his radical band of leftists took us all hostage and initiated their hate-filled takedown of America. You see, according to the mainstream press, there is absolutely nothing to the story about Hunter Biden, his uncle, and the man who is now president of the United States. To them, the story is a sad one about a young man trying to reclaim his life after a downfall from drugs and debauchery, and should be met with nothing more than a yawn and a wave of the hand. They say there's simply nothing there.

Are they correct?

You tell me.

2020: The Swamp Strikes Back

At the end of the 2020 presidential campaign, Joe Biden was exhausted for virtually no reason. And speaking of virtual, the whole "campaign" seemed to emanate from his virtual headquarters via Zoom. After several months spent doing events via video call from his basement in Delaware, his team had finally dragged him out, propped him up, and let him start blathering to his crowds in person—if, of course, you can call a few sad, lonely cars sitting side-by-side in parking lots "crowds." When one of these Biden fans heard something they liked, they responded by blaring their virtual hands, a.k.a. horns.

Let us not forget the one in-person event orchestrated by his crack team that couldn't actually put ten people in the ten circles actually drawn on the floor of the campaign event.

The results had been predictable.

Every time he appeared in public, Biden gave the country all the evidence it needed to suggest that he shouldn't be let within a hundred miles of the White House. During a speech in Delaware, he forgot what office he was running for. A few weeks later, he quoted the Declaration of Independence as saying, "We hold these truths to be self-evident. All men and women are created by the, you know . . . you know, the thing!"[2]

If we only could have known how much worse things would soon get. Considering the events of the past few years, those old gaffes seem like the polished language of a distinguished statesman!

In fact, if the guy hadn't gone on to become the leader of the free world, we might be able to look back on all those quotes and laugh. If old Sleepy Joe had lost the election, packed his things, and gone home to relax on his porch in Delaware, future historians might have been kind to him. They might have written about a senator from Scranton, Pennsylvania, who'd overcome enormous obstacles—finishing near the bottom of his class in law school, for example, or being virtually unable to complete a full sentence—to become vice president of the United States. They'd talk about how he passed some bills, sniffed the heads of some women and girls, and was always in the room when President Barack Obama made his biggest decisions. Compared to all that, his short-lived run for president in 2020 would have been a quick sentence, or maybe even a footnote. As a result of that campaign, being able to complete a sentence is no longer a prerequisite for higher office. Biden shattered that glass ceiling.

If the 2020 election had been conducted like a normal election, that sentence probably would have gone something like this:

"In 2020, after three failed presidential campaigns, Vice President Biden was tapped by members of his party to run against President Donald Trump, but his campaign was derailed at the last moment when it was revealed that Biden's son Hunter had engaged in several nefarious activities, both domestic and foreign, many of which involved his father."

But as you know, that's not what happened. Despite having all the information necessary to prove that Hunter Biden, Joe's youngest son, had engaged in questionable international activities which involved his father both at the inception and the end payouts, the media ignored it.[3] The very organizations that Donald Trump had been elected to fight—the media, Big Tech, and the intelligence community—decided that the 2020 election was their last chance to fight back and ensure their continued survival.

And they fought back *hard.*

During this campaign, all the classic Swamp Creatures made reappearances: John Brennan, the Prince of Darkness who had served as Barack Obama's CIA Director for four years; James Clapper, the director of the NSA who had said, with that admitting look to the Left, that his agency did not spy on American citizens, well—"*not wittingly*," at least; and, of course, Cardinal James Comey, the man without whom none of this nonsense would have been possible.

If all this had appeared in a film script about dirty tricks and political intrigue in Washington, the director might have given it back to the writer and told him to tone it down a little. Even for a gritty political thriller, the director might have said, some of these schemes are a little too far-fetched. Some of the characters seem just a little *too* evil to be real people. Surely, no real person would move this quickly to sell out his country in pursuit of power and the continued dominance of their twisted political ideology. It just doesn't seem possible!

But this was no Hollywood screenplay. This was real life during the election of 2020.

No surprise. This was the election, after all, that came in the wake of devastating lockdowns instated by liberal mayors and governors—lockdowns that had forced thousands of small businesses to close and thousands more people to die, especially seniors forced to live with those infected with the virus. It was the election that occurred after our major cities were still burning and suffering from destruction of those so-called "peaceful protests." The violent race riots, when police officers clashed with protestors who screamed and spit in their faces and attacked them with bike locks and stones. The Left had no problem allowing massive racial justice protests to tear New York City, Chicago, Seattle, Denver, Baltimore, Washington D.C., and other major cities apart. Twenty-five people died during the 2020 protests prompted by the death of George Floyd.[4]

It was the election when the Washington Swamp finally came out and showed the voters of America that it was they, not the people, who are really in charge of our democracy. Over the course of a few weeks in October, the major institutions of this country showed us that when they want to put a candidate in office—even if that candidate is one who has been wrong on every foreign policy issues over his forty-seven-year political career, like Joe Biden—then that candidate will end up in office. It doesn't matter what independent journalists, concerned citizens, or the opposing campaign have to say about it.

What follows is the story that would have been told in the final months of the 2020 election if it hadn't been for this dedicated band of liberal, so-called progressive activists—one that involves sex, drugs, intrigue, and most importantly—corruption of candidate for the highest office in the land who has lied and said he knows nothing of his son's business dealing. Who has already proven he's open to pay to play when as vice president he took that son on Air Force Two to China to meet with Communist Chinese Party–connected officials who would be funding Hunter's business endeavors. All of which should have stopped Joe Biden from ever getting within a hundred blocks of 1600 Pennsylvania Avenue.

It begins, oddly enough, in a computer repair shop in Delaware, where Hunter Biden left his 13-inch MacBook Pro for maintenance in the fall of 2019 and then walked away, never to return.

October Surprise

When John Paul Mac Isaac, the owner of The Mac Shop in Wilmington, Delaware, got Hunter's laptop running again, I'm sure he had to take a shower soon afterward.

According to multiple sources, within the files of this computer were videos and photos that would have made Hugh Hefner blush—from naked photos to crack binges to incriminating characters. Scrolling through the thumbnails, this man would have seen, in no particular order: crack rocks, naked women, trashed hotel rooms, more naked women, more crack rocks, Hunter Biden's penis, more crack rocks, liquid crack, a spoon, *more* naked women, and, finally, some more crack for good measure.

It seemed that every time Hunter Biden decided to buy drugs—something he did with alarming frequency—he brazenly documented every second of the illegal interactions for posterity. I wouldn't be surprised if he brought a full sound system and a documentary crew along with him on some of these shady meetups. Looking through the photos, you would think that he had plans to put together some memorabilia at the end of his adventures, calling the whole thing a Scumbag Scrapbook. Just imagine what Hunter thought was too much for tape? Curiously, there were some photos of Joe Biden with foreign nationals who would later be identified as business associates.

But Mac Isaac had no plans to go public with the information contained on Hunter's laptop. I'm sure that as the proprietor of a computer repair shop, he'd seen plenty of nasty things on plenty of laptops over the years. So, when the laptop was ready, he called Hunter Biden several times to let him know. But his calls were never returned. As we would later learn, Hunter was busy going on a drug-fueled sex binge at the time, having told his family he was going to rehab and then bolting as soon as he was dropped off at the front door of the facility. As anyone who has dropped off a computer knows, if it's not picked up within ninety days it is considered abandoned property. Hunter never went back to pick up that computer and for two years denied it was his.

Meanwhile, Joe Biden was quickly failing to the top. Who could forget Kamala Harris going after him about his opposition to school bussing, something she assured us made Joe a racist!

And he was doing it all as the world learned more and more about Hunter Biden's suspicious dealings in Ukraine. According to information that had long been public, Hunter Biden—a man with no background in energy, no prior experience in the Ukraine, whose father as vice president was the country's point man on energy—received $3 million from Burisma and had been hired by Burisma Energy at a rate of $80,000 per month. Clearly, he was trading on the Biden name, and the people who'd hired him believed he was going to open doors for them.

The question, in the eyes of the public, was which doors? And how was Hunter Biden planning to open them? Was Vice President Joe Biden involved in Hunter's business dealings? And if so, how would his involvement affect national security if he became president? Given that many of Hunter's business deals involved partners in Mexico, Ukraine, and China, these questions were more than fair. They were essential.

Unfortunately, most mainstream media outlets didn't think so. After four years of getting kicked around by President Trump, they were willing to do anything in their power to make sure Trump didn't get a second term. So they ignored the stories about Hunter Biden. For years, whenever a lead showed up, they refused to follow it, leaving the work to smaller outlets with a much more limited audience. All the while, they chased down bogus stories about the Trump family like they would soon lead to the modern incarnation of the Pentagon Papers. If you have any doubt, go ahead and search "Donald Trump Jr." on the website of any major news organization; you're guaranteed to get a few dozen pages of results, many of which predicted he was going to jail any minute. Do the same thing with "Hunter Biden," and you'll probably see a kind, measured review of his latest art show.

As Mac Isaac watched this saga unfold, he knew something was wrong. Right here at his computer repair shop, he had a machine that could potentially contain key evidence in a corruption investigation. A literal treasure trove of photos and emails that any prosecutor would give his or her right hand to get a hold of. Along with Hunter Biden's elicit photos, his laptop also contained every email and text message that he'd sent for the past several years. Even as the world focused on the lurid tales of sex and drugs, it was these emails that held the key to exposing the worst of what Hunter Biden had been up to.

So, having made several attempts to get the laptop back to Hunter and stay out of the whole thing for good, Mac Isaac did what any good citizen would do. He called the FBI and told them what he had. In a month, he met with several FBI agents and showed them the laptop.

But the agents didn't seem in any rush to investigate. In fact, The FBI did not want anything to do with another October Surprise.

Everyone remembered the 2016 fallout that ensued after James Comey—the sanctimonious FBI director who had worked tirelessly against President Trump for years—first announced Hillary was the subject of an investigation in the lead-up to the 2016 election. But shortly before that same election, he then announced no reasonable prosecutor would bring charges against her for the emails in question.

Sensing that the FBI wasn't going to act quickly on the laptop story—if they acted at all—Mac Isaac began looking for other ways to get the story out. Eventually, he sent a copy of the hard drive to

Bob Costello, the lawyer for former Mayor Rudy Giuliani. From Giuliani, the contents of the laptop ended up in the hands of the *New York Post*.

Instead of focusing on the lurid photographs, reporters focused on what mattered: emails between Hunter Biden and his many business associates, which made it clear that among other things, Joe Biden had lied when he said, "I have never spoken to my son about his overseas business dealings."[5]

"Never."

In these emails, reporters at the *Post* found information about deals in China, Ukraine, and Mexico. They found correspondence from several foreign business partners thanking Hunter for introducing them to his father. One Ukrainian official named Vadym Pozharskyi thanked Hunter specifically for "inviting me to DC and giving an opportunity to meet your father and spent [sic] some time together."[6]

These reporters did the kind of work that was once commonplace in newsrooms of every major American newspaper, resulting in a news story which the *New York Post* published at five o'clock in the morning on October 14, 2020.

"Hunter Biden," the first lines read, "introduced his father, then-Vice President Joe Biden, to a top executive at a Ukrainian energy firm less than a year before the elder Biden pressured government officials in Ukraine into firing a prosecutor who was investigating the company, according to emails obtained by The Post."[7]

And on it went from there. That day, less than a month before the presidential election, readers of the *New York Post*—the United States of America's oldest newspaper, founded in the years immediately following the Revolutionary War by Alexander Hamilton— were able to see documented proof that one of the candidates in that election was deeply involved in his son's unethical business dealings. It was a classic October Surprise. In a different, less politically charged era, the *New York Post* might have been in contention for the Pulitzer Prize for their ability to find the story buried within such a dense, nasty trove of digital garbage.

But that's not what happened.

Just hours after the *Post* sent a tweet alerting its two million followers that the story was live, the knives came out. Liberal accounts denounced the story as misinformation. Some even called it "Russian disinformation," relying on the old, stale playbook that had been used against President Trump for four years. By the time the Hunter Biden laptop story hit the internet, there was almost nothing that these people wouldn't label "Russian misinformation."

That same day, Twitter announced it had locked the account of the *New York Post*, citing a violation of its policy on "hacked materials." For a few days, Twitter also locked the accounts of any ordinary Twitter users if they posted the story as a link.

The Democrats moved full throttle to censor the story.

As this ordeal unfolded, the nation got a close look at just how much power Big Tech companies had gained in the past few years alone. When a small body of woke employees at a private company decided they didn't like a single story published by a conservative newspaper, that newspaper was prevented not only from publishing the story in question, but from sending any tweets at all about any topic to the two million people who relied on the paper for information. This did not include the millions of people who would engage in separate conversations about the story.

Meanwhile, left-leaning publications—many of which had spread the now-debunked Steele dossier far and wide for four years with absolutely no complaints from Twitter—were free to denounce the *Post* from their Twitter accounts with reckless abandon. I wonder where this Twitter censorship board was when Edward Snowden was using the platform to post hundreds of stories about critical national security programs, or when a group of investigative journalists published "The Panama Papers," which contained stolen financial information about the world's financial elite.

This policy goes against everything that allows a free press to function.

If Twitter and this policy had been around when the *New York Times* published the Pentagon Papers, for instance—an exposé that remains legendary in the annals of American journalism to this day for its furtherance of the public good—they would have had to shut down the account of the *Times* because the documents contained in the story had been "stolen."

But times had changed. The year was 2020, and the progressives had decided this election was too important to leave to the free choice of a well-informed electorate. They decided they could take the flak for banning a story that was bad for Joe Biden, counting on the fact that everyone would forgive those responsible once he was safely in the White House where they wanted him.

But even Big Tech wasn't enough for them. In their eyes, the 2020 election was far too important to leave in the hands of a few tech companies. For this job, they needed to bring out the big guns.

And they did.

On October 19, while the account of the *New York Post* was still completely locked, more than fifty former senior intelligence officials signed a letter stating—not alleging, not supposing, not theorizing, but *stating*—that the emails contained on Hunter Biden's laptop had "all the classic earmarks of a Russian information operation."[8]

After four years of trying to make this work with absolutely no success, they had to take one final shot at pinning the obvious failings of the Democrat nominee for president on Vladimir Putin and his imaginary cabal of shadowy hackers.

But it worked, as these slimy, reprehensible swamp creatures knew that it would. The mainstream media bought it and then sold it. Just a few hours after the letter emerged from the depths of the Swamp, *Politico* ran a story about it. Then it was quickly picked up by every outlet in the country that had an ax to grind with President Trump—which is to say, *all of them*. Thanks to the status that these legacy publications gave them—not to mention the stamp of approval from more than fifty former intel chiefs—the liberal cabal at Big Tech had all the cover in the world to keep pushing the lie that it was the Russians who'd planted all those messages on Hunter Biden's laptop.

Meanwhile, these same outlets bemoaned the fact that they could not "independently verify" the *Post*'s reporting. They said that although there seemed to be nothing amiss about the messages themselves, there was no way to know whether they were real or not.

Now, I didn't go to school for investigative journalism, but I know how to check whether an email is real or not. So does your average ten-year-old. Even if you can't get Hunter Biden on the phone—which, given how busy he was doing oil paintings at the time, was probably the case—then you could at least reach out to all the people he had supposedly emailed. You could pick up the phone, call the person who'd received the email, and ask a simple question, just like a real journalist: "Did you receive an email from Hunter Biden on this date with this subject line? Yes or no." Or you could ask if you ever took a photo with Vice President Joe Biden.

27

It would have taken no more than a few hours for some team of investigative reporters at the *New York Times* to do this and learn that the emails were real. Given the years of experience that every reporter at that newspaper has, it would have been easier than finding a picture of Hunter Biden's penis on the internet. You can bet all the money in the world that if the emails had come from a laptop belonging to Don Jr., they would have stopped the presses and had everyone in the building on the phone to verify their authenticity for the next day's newspaper—even the janitorial staff. Then again, they wouldn't even bother to try to verify.

But they didn't verify the emails because they didn't *want* to verify the emails, at least not before the presidential election. In their own words, President Trump represented an "existential threat to democracy," and they were willing to do anything to make sure he didn't get another four years in the White House. They knew that eventually, every bit of the reporting that appeared in the *Post* on October 14, 2020, would prove accurate. They just wanted to make sure that it wasn't allowed to happen before Biden was in the White House, right where they wanted him.

It worked.

In November of 2020, Joe Biden won the election. A little over two months later, he stood on the steps of the United States Capitol and took the oath of office. Hunter Biden, dressed in an overcoat and looking as respectable and calm as he could, sat nearby in a chair. Most people watching at home probably had no idea that as he sat watching his father deliver his inaugural address, Hunter was under investigation for potential tax crimes—tax evasion, money laundering, FARA (Foreign Agents Registration Act) violation, false statements, Foreign Corrupt Practice Act. It is important to note that Hunter Biden's wrongdoings are not the end of the story. At issue is his father's role and his alleged involvement in his son's foreign business dealings. Republicans allege that Joe "personally participated in meetings and phone calls" regarding his son's business exploits. "To be clear, Joe Biden is the big guy" according to Rep. James Comer (R-KY)—"we're not trying to prove Hunter Biden is a bad actor. Our investigation is about Joe Biden."[9] The Biden family's financial activity generated more than 150 suspicious bank activity reports.

As of this writing, that investigation is still ongoing. Although Hunter finally admitted the laptop was his, only to have his high-paid Washington D.C. powerhouse lawyer say he really didn't mean that.

And the disclosures about his crooked business dealings haven't stopped. It seems that every day, there is a new leak of documents and photos that reveals the rot at the center of the Biden Crime Syndicate is even deeper than we once believed. In the summer of 2022, I hosted a show on *Fox Nation* titled "Who Is Hunter Biden?" and looked into the question.

Hunter Biden, as I say in the first moments of the series, is both an enigma and an open book. He has written a memoir that talks about the most painful, embarrassing moments of his life, and yet he refuses to acknowledge a child he had with a stripper named Lunden Roberts, a woman who was on the payroll of Hunter's small consulting company during her pregnancy.[10] As we speak, she is in Connecticut having fought to establish paternity with Hunter and won—to give their four-year-old daughter the Biden last name. He talks openly about the love he supposedly had for his brother Beau, and yet his recently uncovered texts and emails reveal a relationship between the two brothers that was far more complicated.

In one of those messages, a rant that stretches to nearly 2,500 words, Hunter describes himself as "the looser [sic] brother always following along behind his super star brother picking up the crumbs he left on the floor." He talks about how all his friends have "always thought of me as a joke and the clown that Beau took care of."[11]

At the moment, it can't really be said that anyone truly knows Hunter Biden or the extent of his crooked business dealings—certainly not his business partners or the three women he's had children with. In her own memoir, published in 2022, Hunter's ex-wife Kathleen Buhle writes that she had to find out from her own teenage daughters that their father was having an affair with Hallie Biden, the widow of his brother Beau.

"How could you have not even suspected?" they asked. "You may have been the only one not to."[12]

Of course the timing of her book gives us a bit more insight. A federal grand jury was impaneled and it was in Kathleen's best interest to communicate to prosecutors publicly, at least, that she knew nothing.

One thing is clear: we've only scratched the surface of what this man has done. No matter how much the Biden White House is willing to lie for this degenerate, sex-crazed scumbag, the truth is going to come out eventually. When you're dealing with this kind of criminal—the one who just can't help himself, even when he's got every advantage in the world, even when the fate of our country is at stake—it always does.

If you need proof of that, just look at the man's life so far.

The Bidens—Joe, Hunter, and even Joe's brother James—were able to prevent the public from reading about that laptop. Joe would continue with the lie that he knew nothing of his son's overseas business dealings and the claim that the laptop had all the earmarks of Russian disinformation persisted.

In a sane, fully-functioning democracy, Joe Biden would have paid dearly for the kinds of statements he made during the lead-up to the midterm elections—if not in the press and the court of public opinion, then at least at the ballot box. There was very little that Biden could tout. The withdrawal from Afghanistan had been a colossal disaster, crime on America's streets was soaring, inflation was at a forty-year high, gas prices were doubled and food prices were tripled, and the border was a disaster.

When election day came, the Democrat Party should have been drowned by a red wave that set records and made the Progressive Left afraid ever to utter vile phrases such as "semi-fascist" again. If the playing field were level, the midterm elections of 2022 would have gone down in history as the most severe (and well-deserved) beat-down ever suffered by one political party at the hands of another.

But that didn't happen.

Instead, Republicans gained only a slim majority in the House of Representatives, while the United States Senate remained blue. The morning after the election was a sober one for Republicans who were shocked at how things had turned out. Somehow, soaring crime rates and record-high inflation had not resulted in the red wave that so many media outlets—liberal ones included—were sure was coming.

In the aftermath, Americans asked why were the Republicans losing on the issues? Did Republicans no longer speak for the American people?

The Democrats, led by the extreme Left of their party, voted on an issue that most thought was in the single digits—abortion. Democrats believe women have the right to abort the unborn at any time during a pregnancy with no restrictions; Republicans, whether pro-life or pro-choice, agreed with the recent Supreme Court's decision with *Dobbs v. Jackson* which held that abortion was not a constitutional issue but one better left to the states. Democrats insist that we prioritize the rights of violent criminals over the rights of victims, enacting ridiculous bail reform laws to ensure these criminals get out of jail as quickly as possible; Republicans want to send violent criminals to prison. Democrats want to tear down our history, while Republicans want to preserve it and teach it to our children. Democrats believe that when an eight-year-old says she thinks she might be a boy in the wrong body, we should encourage that delusion by pumping the child full of off-label drugs and then performing surgery on her; Republicans think that she's just being a kid.

So I think it's safe to say that when it comes to issues, the Republican Party is far more aligned with the American people than the Democrats.

Take the midterm elections, for instance. As election day approached, anyone could see that something was very wrong. The signs were everywhere. The Democrats, for instance, seemed to believe that election day should last a few weeks, not twenty-four hours. In cities and towns all over the country, they passed out mail-in ballots at alarming rates, barely keeping track of who was filling out those ballots or who was collecting them. This gave them an edge over Republicans, who clung to the outdated notion that elections should be held on a single day to ensure a lack of fraud and voter intimidation.

But the mainstream media did not cover this. Instead, they attacked anyone who raised concerns about the potential for misconduct that was created when one party came to rely so heavily on such shady methods of "getting out the vote." The climate for conservatives was so hostile that no one dared question what the Democrats were up to.

According to a study done shortly after the midterm elections, mainstream news outlets aired negative coverage of conservative candidates a stunning 87 percent of the time, compared to just 67 percent for Democrat candidates.

That, folks, is what it looks like when the media picks a side.

For a while, it seemed that the antidote to this outright bias was social media—a place where ordinary Americans could voice their concerns and attempt to shine a light on the stories that traditional media was ignoring. Sometimes, that's exactly what happened.

But over time, it began to seem as if even Twitter—a platform that was supposed to be decentralized and free of bias—was nothing more than the mainstream media times ten thousand. Soon, we saw the same left-wing bias creeping in, and the same absence of any conservative points of view.

It almost seemed as if someone was working from within these companies, particularly Twitter, to make sure the Left could retain its unfair advantage.

There was a time when all this was just rumor and guesswork, of course. People who expressed conservative views on Twitter—especially if those conservative views became popular—would see their follower counts decline for no reason. One post would get millions of views, while the next one would get just a few hundred despite no apparent change in content or style. All we could do was put the pieces together and assume that someone within the company was pulling strings, hiding accounts, and making sure any content that challenged the Left regime was tucked away where no one could see it.

But whenever we would say something, the people who ran Twitter and other tech companies like Facebook would assure us nothing out of the ordinary was going on. They would say that this kind of thing was par for the course, or that audiences simply were not interested in what conservative accounts had to say. Then, like always, the mainstream media would eat up these denials and print them in full, never bothering to look into the allegations themselves. Anyone who insisted they had been "shadowbanned" was viewed as a conspiracy theorist, as was anyone who advocated on behalf of the many conservative accounts that seemed to have been banned from social media for virtually no reason.

Looking back, it's a miracle that the truth about Twitter ever came to light.

But thanks to a billionaire entrepreneur and a few intrepid independent journalists, the truth was revealed, much to the dismay of those who'd been running our social media companies.

Prior Restraint

For a while, the progressives were just fine with Elon Musk. After all, the man was making it possible for ordinary Americans to drive electric cars—something that had once seemed like an environmentalist pipe dream. Sure, he had a lot of money, which tends to annoy them. And he seemed generally pretty happy, which *always* drives them insane. But since he created an electric car powered by a lithium battery, he became the Lefts' superhero.

It wasn't until Musk announced his intention to buy Twitter, the social media company that had become the de facto public square over the past few election cycles, that the leftists rose up, threw down their soy protein smoothies, and started attacking this man like he was, to use their favorite phrases, *a racist and literal Nazi.*

Why?

After all, if Twitter really was the open, unbiased platform that the Left always assured us it was, then a change in ownership of a hero to the Left shouldn't matter at all—*right?* If there was no cabal of left-wing censors working from within that company's headquarters to ensure that only liberal content could be shared widely and discussed, then they should have had nothing to worry about.

But they *were* worried, because they knew exactly what was going on inside the headquarters of this company. They knew, for instance, there was a clear system in place for making sure some accounts did not have the same reach that others did. They knew that certain accounts—nearly all of them conservative—were placed on various "blacklists" within Twitter, making it impossible for ordinary people to find them on their timelines or via the search function.

They also knew that Twitter executives had been lying about it for years. In September of 2018, during his testimony in front of Congress, Twitter CEO Jack Dorsey was asked point-blank whether Twitter was "shadowbanning prominent Republicans."[13] By then, most people were aware that something was going on. But they weren't sure what. And thanks to Twitter's status as a private company, the world had to take Dorsey at his word.

His answer?

"No."

That same year, speaking with Brian Stelter on CNN, Dorsey said, "If someone puts out a tweet, [are we] hiding that tweet from everyone without that person who tweeted it knowing about it? The real . . . question is, are we doing something according to political ideology or viewpoints? And we are not, period."[14]

Well, Jack, it looks like your lies have finally caught up to you. Now might be a good time to take another one of your silent yoga retreats in the desert, because *a lot* of people are going to want you to start talking.

Almost as soon as Elon Musk took over—an event that incited a full-on meltdown from the mainstream press, of course—we began to see exactly how much Jack Dorsey and the old Twitter mafia had distorted reality, buried the truth, and influenced our elections to make sure their chosen candidates could not lose.

It should go without saying, of course, that each and every one of those chosen candidates was a Democrat. As the independent journalist Michael Shellenberger would point out in Part Three of the "Twitter Files," more than 96 percent of political donations made by employees at Twitter went to Democrat candidates in 2018, 2020, and 2022.[15]

Our electoral system is predicated on fairness. When one side is artificially suppressed—especially when it is suppressed by a private company that claims complete neutrality when it comes to matters of politics—we become no better than a banana republic in which one regime, no matter what the opinion polling says, always seems to come out on top when the votes are counted on election night.

As journalists kept digging through the internal papers at Twitter—what would soon come to be known as the "Twitter Files"—the truth got even stranger and more outrageous. They found, for instance, there was an incestuous relationship between the employees of Twitter and the FBI, where the FBI warned Twitter that incoming hacked information about Hunter Biden from Russia would be leaked. First, there was the fact that James Baker—the lawyer who had overseen the Russia Collusion Delusion during his time at the Bureau—was attempting to stop publication of all Twitter files.[16] (He failed, of course.)

Then there was the sheer audacity of the operation. For years, it seemed that whenever the FBI wanted someone gone—and, as always, these "undesirables" were conservatives—they would send a quick message to Twitter, which would then promptly remove them from the platform or make it so their content was invisible to users. In the lead-up to our elections, one side was overrepresented while the other side was being suppressed by the government.

This was especially true when it came to Covid-19, the greatest gift the Democrats ever got.

The Origins of Totalitarianism

We saw what the Left was capable of during the first months of Covid-19. We saw exactly where their priorities were as they shut down churches, community centers, small businesses, and nursing homes all while allowing strip clubs, casinos, and liquor stores to remain open as "essential businesses." We watched a father hauled off in handcuffs for the crime of playing catch outdoors with his son during lockdown, and we saw a hairdresser was sentenced to jail for trying to work.

People wanted to work. But the state governments would not let them. In San Diego, Pastor Rob McCoy felt he had no choice other than to reclassify his church as a "family-friendly strip club" so that the state of California would allow him to preach.[17]

Then, in November of 2020, the radicals gained more power than anyone ever expected them to get. With Joe Biden and his handlers in the White House, the worst authoritarian tendencies of the Left went mainstream. One of their first acts in office was to find anyone spreading Covid "misinformation," hunt them down, and take them out. Their accomplices, of course, were the employees of Twitter, who have always been happy to help the government suppress the free speech of ordinary Americans—especially when those ordinary Americans were speaking out against them. During their first few months in office, Biden, the Trojan Horse candidate, released his far-left goons and succeeded in removing anyone who dared go against the party line on Covid—journalists, doctors, and respected epidemiologists among them.

And it wasn't only the social media companies.

As one of his first acts in office, Biden worked behind the scenes to create his own Ministry of Truth, a group that would work under the umbrella of the Department of Homeland Security to sift through online "misinformation." When it came time to pick someone to do the job, Biden headed (presumably) to an alley behind a Broadway theater and found a telepathic genius named Nina Jankowicz who wrote books and articles claiming that the Russians helped elect Donald Trump, that the Steele dossier was full of real information, and that the Hunter Biden laptop was nothing more than "Russian disinformation."[18]

Does all that election denial and disinformation-spreading make her a "threat to democracy"? Did the censorship team at Twitter—a team led by the former FBI lawyer James Baker, Cardinal James Comey's right-hand man—decide that her account should be shadowbanned or deleted entirely?

No. She was on the right team.

In August, Baker's old buddies at the FBI raided the home of former president Donald J. Trump because, in their opinion, that president had mishandled classified documents and stored them in the wrong place. Meanwhile, Hillary Clinton—who used a private email server to handle classified documents when she was Secretary of State, among a few thousand other sins—had not received so much as a phone call from the corrupt, conservative-hating agents of the FBI other than to tell her all was good with them. As of this writing, she continues to sell T-shirts and hats reading "But Her Emails," raking in big bucks in the process, maybe even more than the cattle futures profits.

These people will not stop the labeling of certain facts "misinformation," thereby making them disappear from the public so they won't have to deal with them. They attempt to label the *people* who share that "misinformation" with a whole host of claims—racist, Nazis, right-wing extremist. Biden's moronic "semi-fascist" address was just the beginning. As the months of Joe Biden's term go on, we are sure to see more name-calling, hate, and relentless attacks from the Biden administration, the members of which so often claim to be the "adults in the room."

Since Trump, look at the disasters the "adults" brought you:

- Calamitous Afghanistan withdrawal
- 40-year high inflation
- Involvement in war in Ukraine
- Gas, groceries, and basic utility prices skyrocketing
- A national unaddressed crime spree
- Anarchy at the southern border
- A loss of respect for the United States on the world stage

But thanks to the coordination of Big Tech, mainstream media, and the intelligence community, Biden and his cronies were not punished for these crimes. Instead, they have been rewarded with votes and accolades from the press.

As we move forward, I'm sure that the Left's Spin Machine will kick into overdrive to obscure, bury, or outright erase all negative stories about Joe Biden and his puppet masters. If they have their way, Googling the words "Hunter Biden" will yield nothing more than a few selfies and links to buy all that great "art" he's been working on. Poking around social media for information about the Biden family's deals with Chinese financial conglomerates will lead you to links for Chinese restaurant menus and nothing more.

Even in the aftermath of the Twitter Files—which, of course, mainstream news outlets have labeled a "nothing-burger" and a "conspiracy theory" despite voluminous evidence that Big Tech has been in league with Democrats for years—the Radical Left is attempting to make us forget all about the corruption of the Biden family. Hopefully with the Republicans in power, there will be some truth-finding—although without an objective Department of Justice, we will probably never see real justice as in prosecutions.

The Trojan Horse

When Congressman James Clyburn, House Majority Whip from South Carolina and the highest-ranking African American in Congress, gave the crucial thumbs-up to Joe Biden just before his state's primary, effectively handing him the nomination as well as the seal of approval among black voters, many warned Clyburn was empowering a Trojan Horse. There were those who believed that despite his moderate background and his age, hidden inside his Trojan Horse were far-left, socialist-loving, leftist radicals to whom he would ultimately cave.

The truth is that even with the president, it's not simply the name on the ballot that matters. What matters is the power he gives to people around him. Who are the people who brief him? Who are the people that support him? Who are the people he asks opinions of? These are the people that matter. Joe surrounded himself with an army of hungry young socialists who lined up behind him—the people who took their first gender studies course during the Obama years. These are the people with a plan to shut down the fossil fuel industry. They're the ones who tell white children they are responsible for slavery, the ones who think our children should be able to change genders without parental notification, the ones who take a knee when the National Anthem is being played.

And thanks to the unprecedented intervention by Big Tech, the media, and the intelligence community in October of 2020, they are now all in the White House.

It was never about Joe Biden. Nobody has ever been passionate about him, and that was never more true than in 2020. Biden was simply the vehicle. His vehicle, the Trojan Horse, rolled up to the front gate of America, while the Radical Left hid inside with their secret agenda. Once Biden was in control, they jumped out, shunted him into a White House closet or back to Delaware where he has so far spent one quarter of his presidency, and proceeded to implement their vision for America.

That America, under Biden was a different America. It was an America that tolerated out-of-control crime. It was an America that tolerated the loss of sovereignty. It was an America that was willing to go on bended knee to our enemies for energy. There was no America First, or proud to be an American agenda. His Trojan Horse brought with it an acceptance of the Left's most progressive agenda—turning America into the most left-leaning, progressive country it had ever been. To use a turn of a Barack Obama's phrase, "Joe Biden did that." For the first time, a whole swath of Americans was made to feel they were not only not a part of the American dream, but that dream was more out of reach for them than ever. And if they felt like outliers as a result of Biden's derision and downright hatred, that was the intent.

It seemed that America was more welcoming of illegal immigrants who swore no allegiance to Her than the American citizens who did, who toiled hard, paid their taxes, followed the law, and believed in Her.

On day one in the Oval Office, Joe Biden signed an executive order canceling the permit of the Keystone XL Oil and Gas Pipeline along with eleven thousand jobs connected to that pipeline. Keeping the permit in place was inconsistent with his climate imperative, Biden said. That pipeline was to carry millions of gallons of oil from Canada to refineries in the U.S. Along with that cancellation, the executive order revoked oil and gas development at national wildlife monuments. During his first 100 days, he also canceled several oil and gas leases in the Gulf of Mexico and elsewhere, severely limiting the ability of our energy companies to produce fuel. The takedown of America's energy independence had begun. But the cancellation had even broader implications. The leadership of Canada's Alberta province, where oil is a major part of its economy, called Biden's decision an "insult" and recommended the Canadian government impose trade sanctions if the pipeline construction were to remain halted.

As the United States suffers an invasion of millions of illegal immigrants from more than 140 countries, we are literally absorbing people about whom we know nothing. One would never have expected this to occur during the administration of a president who once spoke about jailing employers who hired illegals, who said sanctuary cities should not be allowed to violate federal law, and bragged about voting for the Secure Fence Act.

As a speaker in 2006 at a South Carolina rotary club, Biden praised the bill that authorized 700 miles of double-layered fence along the southern border with more than a billion dollars in appropriations. In the speech he was emphatic "and let me tell you something folks, people are driving across that border with tons, tons, hear me, tons of everything from byproducts for methamphetamine to cocaine to heroin and it's all coming up through corrupt Mexico."[1] During the 2008 presidential election, Biden was unsupportive in granting driver's licenses to undocumented immigrants.

The leftist changed all that. We are now living in an unprecedented moment in American history where the president of the United States has indicated that the border is "not a priority" because he has other issues to deal with. Whether it is a conscious disregard for the laws of the United States, or an intentional violation of those federal laws, this president has chosen to allow this country with all its unearned benefits to be home to anyone who so chooses.

They come in caravans of thousands. We watch as they travel from the Central Americas through Mexico and march into the United States. No one is stopping them. The only people who are stopped are the ones who apply to come here legally. The ones who wait in line and follow our rules are put through the ringer physically, financially, and emotionally. But those who violate our laws are rewarded. The message is clear—come to America, we will help you start a new life by providing you with housing, education, medication, a cellphone, and if you make it to New York City, free laundry service, televisions, and babysitters.

No leader with any sense of responsibility to his people would allow this unmitigated effrontery while Americans are locked down in their homes, forced to wear masks (and shamed if they didn't), and forced to prove they were vaccinated in order to keep their jobs. The illegals were made part of a privileged class by the Biden administration. They didn't have to wear masks; they didn't even have to be tested. If they didn't want a vaccination, they didn't have to have one. They were sent into the interior of the United States to spread whatever illness they might have without any regard for Americans who were forced to live under the Left's totalitarian rules.

Joe Biden, "Mr. Moderate," not only allows this to happen, he fights an order that would allow the removal of persons who arrive here from a country where a communicable disease is present! His goal is to let everyone in no matter the risk. There's nothing moderate or fair about border towns being overrun by illegals who have no place to go. Some have simply come to get a job, to take care of their families. There's nothing humane about immigrants being forced to sleep on the streets in Texas without blankets, without coats. The Biden administration, although welcoming the invasion, is not prepared to, or refuses to, deal with these immigrants on a humanitarian level.

Americans watch this invasion in shock, wondering where is border patrol? Why is there no control? Why am I paying for all this? Why is it that mothers who are illegal get baby formula delivered to them on pallets while store shelves in grocery stores and pharmacies are empty of that formula? Why are they treated better than Americans? The answer from the White House that created this formula shortage is that the law requires we have formula for illegal babies. Really? American babies take second place to illegals?

Biden's minions always come out and double down on his lies. Take for example, Karine Jean-Pierre who insisted the border was not open, and that anyone suggesting otherwise was doing the work of human smugglers. She claimed that anyone who suggests the border is open is spreading "misinformation."[2] Yet the U.S. Customs and Border Patrol reported over 2.5 million border encounters in fiscal year 2022,[3] not including the approximately 900,000 "gotaways." So if over 3 million came through the southern border in one year, either Karine or Customs is lying. They can't both be right.

The Biden administration has also directed the Department of Justice to send out the FBI to investigate parents who protested critical race theory in their children's schools. One parent who tried to complain about his daughter being sexually assaulted in school by a male student who identified as a female on a particular day was arrested and taken into custody. The FBI began visiting and interrogating these parents. There is nothing that quells protest like a knock at your door and a visit from your friendly FBI. That the Attorney General of the United States would send a memo to the FBI describing American parents concerned about their children's education as domestic terrorists is about as un-American as it gets.

And when the facts were not in the administration's favor, the Biden crew decided they would just change what is fact and what is fiction. In 2022 they tried to start a disinformation governance board to police against "misinformation"—specifically about immigration and Covid. To lead this new board, they appointed journalist Nina Jankowicz whose chief qualification was that she made a video singing a tune from Mary Poppins to lyrics about misinformation. Ms. Jankowicz, an election denier herself, has repeatedly called into question the legitimacy of the Hunter Biden laptop story, saying it should be viewed as a Trump campaign product.[4] These are the people who always talk about the danger to democracy, yet show their bona fides by appointing a person who pushed disinformation herself. The Left's Ministry of Information and their effort to shut down the truth fortunately was so absurd that even they couldn't justify it and it never really got off the ground.

But the administration knew where to put money to help the American people. They spent taxpayer money on inane projects like sending out "safe smoking kits" that contained crack pipes (hey, thanks to Hunter, they'd have no trouble learning how to use them!).

As opposed to trying to stop the entrance of drugs at the southern border or recognizing that 90 percent of the heroin in this country, and half of the fentanyl, is coming through the open southern border. In fact, although fentanyl kills one hundred Americans every day, Biden never even said the word until two years after he was in office, and 200,000 Americans had died from it.

Economic Euthanasia

Biden is not governing like the moderate within the Trojan Horse. He lies. Remember his address to the AFL-CIO convention in Philadelphia on June 14, 2022. Over the course of just under five thousand words, Biden outright lied about what had happened to ordinary Americans during his brief time in office, as if he knew (and he probably did) no one from the mainstream media would ever dare call him out.

The lies began with Biden's claim that, since he had taken office, "families are carrying less debt nationwide. They have more savings nationwide."[5]

Mark Twain once said, "There are lies, damned lies, and statistics." That one was in the middle category.

According to data from the Federal Reserve, "household debt has increased by over $1.5 trillion since Biden took office in January 2021." Credit card debt is at a record high of $1.103 trillion. The average American savings account shrank from $73,100 in 2021 to $62,086 a year later, even as dramatic inflation made those dollars worth less.[6]

Joe Biden is more language impaired than he is language fluent, and more often than not he puts his foot in his mouth. The question is whether it's his own foot or someone else's that he puts in his mouth. The man has plagiarized speeches for much of his career causing him to drop out of the 1998 presidential race.[7] He's lied about his school record; he's even lied about where he even went to school. But, according to Jill, his long-suffering wife (or the mastermind who drags him around on a leash), it's "just Joe." But there's no consequence. He just keeps lying to the American people.

In a June 8, 2022, appearance on ABC's *Jimmy Kimmel Live!*, Biden boasted, "We have the fastest-growing economy in the world." Then, to make sure you didn't miss it, he repeated it twice: "The world. The world."[8]

Well, it took me about ten seconds of Googling to find out *that* howler wasn't true. In fact, at the time Biden made his remarks, more than *fifty* of the world's countries were enjoying faster growth than America. Colombia, one of the drug capitals of the world, has a faster growing economy than we do. So does Chile. So do Ireland, India, Greece, France, Italy, Panama, the Dominican Republic, and—of course—China, whose steady economic growth was eased along by the Biden administration allowing it to purchase a million barrels of oil from our strategic reserves on the open market, even as Americans suffered through an energy crisis.

From June 2021 to June 2022, the U.S. inflation rate was 9.1 percent, the highest figure in forty years.[9] With inflation that high, Americans were paying a de facto tax of $717 *per month,* just from the steady drop in what their hard-earned dollars could buy.

If Biden had wanted to slow down that inflation burning up Americans' cash savings, he might have considered taking the shackles off of U.S. energy production. But thanks to the left-wing cabal controlling his domestic policy, that was impossible. So instead, like a beggar seeking alms, Biden had to ask the King of Saudi Arabia to bail him out. In mid-October 2022, the kingdom released a statement that the Biden administration had begged them to delay a planned OPEC production cut by one more month. The only purpose of that request: hiding from Americans how enfeebled their own oil production had become just a few more weeks, until the midterm elections were past. Instead, the kingdom told Biden to pound sand (after all, they have plenty of it). So much for Biden's approximately two centuries of foreign policy experience that supposedly qualified him for the White House. How long before he starts begging the Iranian mullahs for oil instead?

This administration is committing economic euthanasia. Our economy has all the ingredients needed to thrive, but instead of letting it do so, the Biden regime is killing it. And in the process, it is killing Americans as well.

It's no wonder 88 percent of Americans think the country is heading in the wrong direction.[10] Now, it's worth asking ourselves: Who are these 12 percent of people who think the country is headed in the *right* direction? Are they on drugs? Did they not understand the question? Or do they take a glance at generationally high inflation, fuel shortages, and literal truckloads of dead migrants at the border and genuinely think *Yes, that's amazing, I'd like some more, please.*

Sadly, that interpretation may well be the correct one. The sad fact is that many of these people are not only okay with the demise of the United States of America; they're happy about it. They have been taught for years that the United States is an irredeemably evil, systemically racist place. They've consumed a steady diet of anti-American dreck like Nikole Hannah-Jones's *The 1619 Project*, writings that reduce America to a grotesque villain of history, built atop "white supremacy" and noteworthy only for slavery, lynching, and Jim Crow.

To people with such a worldview, America's steady decline can only be something to celebrate. The country is not a cherished heirloom to be protected, nurtured, and improved. Instead, it is a hated symbol of oppression, which can be redeemed only through the destruction and twisted rebirth of its most fundamental institutions. In their eyes, the new version will be better. Instead of capitalism, we'll have neo-Marxism. Instead of merit, we'll have strict quotas on race, gender, and sexual orientation. All men (and women, and nonbinary) will be created equal . . . but some will be more equal than others.

Kamala

Alongside Joe Biden and his leftists in the Trojan Horse was the great Kamala Harris. During her term as United States Senator, she likened ICE to the KKK.[11] She was clearly an alarmingly left-leaning radical vice president. But more than that, she was a joke. At every opportunity she's had to impress the American public, or on the world stage to impress our international allies, she has failed. The woman literally makes no sense when she speaks. I'm tired of her whining, nonsensical, salad sentences which are impossible to diagram, and even harder to comprehend. I'm really tired of her piercing, maniacal laugh that comes out of nowhere for no reason. Every time I hear that laugh I wonder if Kamala's political career sidetracked her from her real dream of playing one of the hyenas in *The Lion King* movie.

Most of all, I am tired of the smug, arrogant way that this woman—who did about as well in the primaries as her boss would do on an IQ test—talks down to the rest of the country from her unearned perch of power. A perch she attained by dating married California Assembly Speaker Willie Brown—thirty years older than she. Kamala Harris, the first woman to ever become vice president, could be a model for young girls of all political affiliations, from all walks of life. Instead, we have a walking diversity checkbox who is unlikeable, unprepared, incapable, and seemingly just doesn't give a damn. The mass exodus of staff from Kamala's personal office—seventeen to date, including Symone Sanders, one of the toughest women in Washington—is rivaled only by the mass exodus over our border from Mexico. Lest we forget, Biden put Kamala in charge of the border—his own special way of announcing *nobody* was in charge of it. Apparently, her smiling and laughing on stage doesn't extend to her office and her staff. She has literally broken the record for the number of people who have quit working with her as vice president. According to them, as a result of her haughtiness, intolerance, and rudeness, Kamala is a nightmare to work for.

According to *Insider*, Kamala's own legion of ex-staff members see her potential rise to the presidency as a "nightmare scenario."[12] Yet that is precisely what Democrats may be stuck with: A choice between their senile Trojan Horse or his cackling affirmative action underling.

But that is what happens when a party doesn't pick its leaders to lead, but simply act as decoys. Joe Biden has never really been in charge, and Kamala Harris never will be either. They are just the battering rams the Radical Left used to break down the doors. But for how long can the Democratic Party get the press to cover this up?

Pay to Play

Hunter Biden is the centerpiece of a pay-to-play empire that has fueled the Biden family for decades, allowing them to live like aristocrats even as their leading figures collect the middling salaries of "public servants." After all, even Joe's wife "Doctor Jill" is a schoolteacher who, by the way, doesn't really have a PhD. She has an EdD, a far cry from a PhD.

Thanks to Hunter's laptop, we have a remarkably complete vision of the most degenerate Biden's business dealings. Yet at the same time, the parts of those dealings that were left unwritten are the final tantalizing piece of a vast puzzle.

As of this writing, not every piece of the Hunter Biden puzzle has been found. But I believe they soon will be. What has already been dug up is simply too overwhelming to brush away. Hunter's behavior, with a laptop corroborating it, is more than sufficient to land him in prison for many years. However, the most pressing issue is not so much Hunter Biden, as it is the president of the United States and his role in the Hunter Biden escapades. How much did he know, what did know, who did he know, and who did he meet with? And now that he is president of the United States, his foreign policy, even our economic future, is tied to countries from which Hunter Biden, and ultimately Joe Biden, have benefitted. The questions about this pay-to-play are at the center of the Biden presidency.

The Left moved heaven, earth, and cyberspace to keep Hunter Biden's laptop and its contents under wraps long enough to get his dad safely into the White House. During that drama, the actual laptop was just a symbol. It could have been anything. What mattered was that Big Tech, the press, Democrats, and the deep state intelligence agencies collectively decided the public shouldn't see it.

But of course, Hunter Biden's laptop is *not* just a symbol. The contents matter. And no, I don't simply mean all the evidence of sex and drugs, however titillating it might be and however many copies of the *New York Post* it helped to sell.

The sleazy life of a sex-crazed loser is not the purpose of this chapter. Hunter's sordid life might reflect badly on Joe Biden's own parenting style, but his personal life is ultimately his own responsibility. What matters for the entire country is the evidence of everything *else*. What matters to a prosecutor is the treasure trove of evidence, both direct and circumstantial, within that laptop.

Every piece of evidence from Hunter's personal life (and thanks to the laptop, we have more pieces than for any person who has ever lived) point toward a man fundamentally incapable of a full, honest day's work. Yet Hunter, the most degenerate Biden, has still had a life of astonishing professional success. He has collected millions in salary, sat on assorted boards, held titled positions with prestigious firms. The question is, how?

Biden, Inc.

In 2021, Hunter was paid a reported $2 million to "write" a memoir, titled *Beautiful Things*. It wasn't a book of photography. It wasn't meeting Gallery Books's bottom line, as the book managed just 10,000 sales in its first week on the market.

Near the beginning of his memoir, Hunter says one of his first memories is of the day he woke up next to his older brother Beau in a hospital room. His father had just been elected to the United States Senate at the age of twenty-nine. His mother, meanwhile, had just died in a car accident—the same accident that left Hunter and his brother in the hospital while their father interviewed staff for his new Senate office.

From there, he writes, things only got worse.

Throughout his childhood, Hunter always felt like he was living in the shadows of his older brother, and for good reason. While Beau was getting good grades and playing soccer on his high school team, Hunter was starting brawls at football games with people who made fun of his dad. He was also beginning to dabble in cocaine—a drug that would follow him continuously. While still in high school, he was arrested for cocaine possession on the Jersey Shore.

But that didn't stop him. Being a senator's son had its perks, and Hunter still gained admission into Georgetown University. During his senior year, Hunter met a homeless crack dealer named Bicycles, who would come to figure prominently in his life. Together, these two began a journey of drugs and debauchery that continues to this day. (In fact, if history is any indication, they're probably sprawled out on two motel beds right now, weighing up crack and preparing to cut deals with Chinese oligarchs.)

When Hunter applied to Yale Law School, likely in a drug-induced haze, he was rejected. So, he enrolled at Georgetown Law as a first-year law student. While all this was happening, Hunter's father was chairing the Senate Judiciary Committee, presiding over the confirmation of judges who hailed from the very Ivy League system to which Hunter was attempting to gain access. The confirmation process, as anyone who follows news about the Senate will know, involves many private, one-on-one interviews with judicial nominees, during which all manner of deals can be struck.

While Joe was the single most powerful member of Congress for weighing judicial nominees, Hunter submitted a transfer application to Yale Law, the nation's most elite law school. His application included a poem detailing his ambition to attend the school, something I'm sure would have set off the admissions department's Psycho Alarm immediately if it had been from anyone besides the son of a powerful U.S. senator. Fortunately, it *was* from a senator's son. So just like his paintings almost three decades later, Hunter's passed muster, and he won admission to Yale. Perhaps miraculously, he finished on time two years later in 1996, the same year his father began a fifth term as U.S. senator.

And *that* is when the real fun began for Hunter. Fresh out of law school, Hunter scored a plum job at MBNA, one of the largest banks in Delaware, paying $100,000 per year (in the days before Joe Biden's 9% inflation, a six-figure starting salary was still an incredible amount). In a remarkable coincidence, MBNA was one of the largest donors to Joe's Senate campaigns.

Of course, just calling MBNA a "large bank" misses the company's actual business model. MBNA was a pioneer in the credit card industry, specializing in offering "affinity cards" bearing the brand of a university, a sports team, or a civic organization. MBNA's ultimate business model, of course, was getting people into a cycle of debt which they then found it hard to escape.

Throughout his career, Biden consistently looked out for MBNA, and MBNA looked out for him. In the words of *Mother Jones* magazine:

> [Biden] brought in more than $200,000 from MBNA employees over the course of his career. And he developed a relationship with the company's CEO, Charles Cawley. When Biden held a Wilmington fundraiser for his 1996 campaign, Cawley was there. When Cawley received an award for his charitable giving, Biden and [George W.] Bush appeared onstage with him. A couple years later, Cawley co-chaired an award ceremony for Biden. On the company's dime, Biden and his wife, Jill, flew to Maine, where the senator spoke at MBNA'S 1997 corporate retreat.[1]

In 2005, Biden supported legislation making it much harder for consumers—say, those using MBNA credit cards—to file for bankruptcy, saving the bank millions.

Biden played ball for MBNA, and in return his druggie son got a plum job straight out of law school . . . and it wasn't even one requiring a law degree! But all this favoritism, it seems, came with a price for Hunter himself. As once-private emails and texts have made clear, Hunter was often a piggy bank for the rest of his family, and frequently grew resentful about it.

In 2019, Hunter texted Naomi Biden, his daughter, whining that he had paid "for everything for this entire family for thirty years." Hunter told Naomi not to worry about her own financial future, because "unlike Pop, I won't make you give me half your salary."

Who is Pop? You know, as do I, as does everyone. It's none other than Old Joe himself. Other emails found on Hunter's laptop detail expenses related to Joe's lakefront Wilmington home that Hunter was responsible for paying off. And no, it wasn't because Hunter crashed a car through the wall while high on coke. According to an email from 2010, Hunter's responsibilities covered everything from $1,239 to fix the air condition in "mom-mom's cottage," to $1,475 for a house painter, to $475 for shutters. There was also a $2,600 bill to repair a stone retaining wall at the lake . . . okay, maybe that one *was* from a Hunter bender.

Somehow, the least capable, most troubled member of the Biden family was the one forking over thousands of dollars to meet expenses. Was this really just the munificence of a successful son? Or a more explicit arrangement: The son too messed up to ever be a politician was instead handed do-nothing sinecures that could finance the family's lifestyle.

For the Bidens, corruption has always been a family affair. It should come as no surprise to anyone that Jim Biden, Joe's brother, pulled Hunter into a family side hustle, tiny meth teeth and all.

For a while, that operation was known to the world as Paradigm Global Advisors, a hedge fund that Jim and Hunter purchased together in 2006. According to an article in *Politico* published shortly after the acquisition, Jim Biden walked in on his first day and told Paradigm's employees, "Don't worry about investors. We've got people all around the world who want to invest in Joe Biden."[2]

The article goes on to say that Jim Biden "made it clear that he viewed the fund as a way to take money from rich foreigners who could not legally give money to his older brother or his campaign account."

"We've got investors lined up in a line of 747s filled with cash ready to invest in the company," Jim reportedly said to one of the fund's executives.[3]

But it turned out that running a real hedge fund was a little harder than being handed one job at a major bank. Within four years, Jim and Hunter had run the hedge fund into the ground. Apparently, "give me bags of money because my brother is a senator" wasn't the bulletproof pitch they thought it was. After several lawsuits from associates, audits from the IRS, and a revelation that the hedge fund's offices were owned by individuals with ties to the government of Iran, Jim and Hunter Biden closed up shop at Paradigm in 2010.

Fortunately for Hunter, he had other options. According to his memoir, he was sober during these years, and had been since about 2003. Apparently, the quick break from drugs and booze gave him more time to figure out how best to use his influence to make money.

In July of 2007, the Biden campaign paid Hunter Biden's law firm just over $20,000 for "legal services." By the end of Biden's presidential bid, according to *National Review*, his campaign had paid Hunter's law firm $143,000 for these "services."

Hunter had agreed to certain restrictions on lobbying when his father became Barack Obama's running mate, but it turns out there was "an unusual loophole in Hunter Biden's refusal to lobby his father." According to a report in the *Washington Post*, "Senator Barack Obama sought more than $3.4 million in congressional earmarks for clients of the lobbyist son of his Democratic running mate. . . . Obama succeeded in getting $192,000 for one of the clients, St. Xavier University in suburban Chicago."[4] Also, as noted in the *Washington Post*, other lobbyists at Biden's firm lobbied his father.⁵ By September of 2008, when Hunter Biden agreed to end his lobbying activities for all clients, the Obama campaign was already very worried about the complications that would come from the work Hunter had already done.

Offshore Accounts

They were also worried about what he would do next—and for good reason.

In June of 2009, just five months after Joe Biden was sworn in as vice president, Hunter founded a new company called Rosemont Seneca Partners with Christopher Heinz, the stepson of John Kerry. The third partner in this venture was Devon Archer, a good friend of Heinz from their days at Yale who would soon become one of Hunter Biden's favorite pen pals.

In messages recovered from Hunter's laptop, you can practically feel the excitement that these two idiots felt while they cut deals overseas with foreign oligarchs. In 2013, Hunter forwarded an article to Devon Archer that claimed Vice President Biden was going to "take on [an] expanded role in foreign policy" during Obama's second term. In the subject line of that email, Hunter wrote: "If we can't figure this out we should be shot."⁶

Soon after Rosemont Seneca's creation, boosted by foreigners' desire to curry favor with the Obama presidency, business was booming for the Bidens.

Of course, it didn't take many of these cool, overseas adventures to get Hunter Biden hooked on drugs again—and booze, and porn, and prostitutes. Hunter had once placated his wife, Kathleen, by telling her he *only* cheated on her while out of the country—and then, only with prostitutes (perhaps he thought this would make his wife *less angry*). But even this proved to be a lie. Not only did Hunter lapse back into drugs, they trended harder, with Hunter dabbling in more cocaine than ever during his frequent trips abroad.

But for Hunter, business was simple. He could afford the distractions. Believe it or not, the phrase "give me bags of money, my father is Vice President" wasn't a hard pitch to memorize, and it was often all he needed to say to get a meeting and close his deals. Jim Biden might have been too incompetent to take advantage, but there really were people all around the world eager to "invest in" Joe Biden.

And many of them, as it turned out, were members of the Chinese Communist Party.

In *Secret Empires*, the journalist Peter Schweizer writes:

> Less than a year after opening Rosemont Seneca's doors, Hunter Biden and Devon Archer were in China having secured access at the highest levels. Thornton Group's account of the meeting on their Chinese-language website is telling: Chinese executives "extended their warm welcome" to the "Thornton Group, with its U.S. partner Rosemont Seneca chairman Hunter Biden (second son of the now Vice President Joe Biden)." The purpose of the meetings was to "explore the possibility of commercial cooperation and opportunity." Curiously, details about the meeting did not appear on their English-language website.[7]

If Hunter and his business partners had just stuck to secret, backdoor meetings with the Chinese, he might have gotten away with his corrupt dealings. He certainly wouldn't have invited the scrutiny of the Obama White House, which had so far shown that it was more than willing to overlook his illicit activities to protect the reputation of its vice president. But Hunter Biden had never been satisfied by playing it safe—or keeping things legal. When it came to shady business deals, he had the same policy as he did with drugs, women, and online pornography: *more, more, more.*

In December of 2013, Hunter accompanied his father on Air Force Two for a trip to China—a move that, according to a *New Yorker* profile of Hunter, made several members of the vice president's office wonder whether Hunter was profiting via access to his father. According to this same profile, none of these Biden aides said anything for fear of inviting ire from the vice president. "Everyone who works for him," one aide said, "has been screamed at."[8] (I should note that in 2019, when this profile was published, the aides in question were probably talking about Biden screaming *at them* in a way meant to be intimidating, not just screaming "C'mon, man!" into the distance as he does now.)

During their trip to China, Hunter arranged a photo op for Vice President Biden with his Chinese business partner Jonathan Li, who ran a private-equity fund in China. And just like everyone who runs a business in China, Li was effectively working as an arm of the Chinese Communist Party, which had just come under the murderous rule of President Xi Jinping.

"Less than two weeks later," noted Peter Schweizer in the *New York Post*, "Hunter Biden's firm inked a $1 billion private equity deal with a subsidiary of the Chinese government's Bank of China. The deal was later expanded to $1.5 billion. In short, the Chinese government funded a business that it co-owned along with the son of a sitting vice president."[9]

All the while, Hunter's drug use kept getting worse and worse. In 2014, less than one year after Vice President Biden pulled strings to get Hunter into the United States Naval Reserves, he was discharged when he failed a drug test, having tested positive for cocaine.[10]

According to photos and messages pulled from the laptop, Hunter also abused alcohol and crack, often doing so in seedy motel rooms all over the world.

But he wasn't done trading on his father's name. In fact, he was just getting started.

As Obama moved into his second term, his vice president had become the White House's point man on China, Ukraine, and many other foreign countries. It makes sense. Given the man's advanced age and already rapidly-declining cognitive skills, who can blame the White House for wanting him out of the country as much as possible? And for Obama at the time, no doubt, the countries he was taking the lead on seemed like reasonable choices. China wasn't a threat, but rather a business opportunity. And Ukraine? Ukraine was just a small, struggling former Soviet nation with a corruption problem even the *New York Times* admitted was "pervasive."

Another place where corruption had been "pervasive" for years? The Biden household. Soon, courtesy of Hunter Biden, the two would cross paths.

Negative Energy

In late 2013, Ukraine was rocked by protests and political upheaval. Protestors took to the streets in Kyiv demanding an end to corruption and closer ties with the west. In February of 2014, after more than eighty people had died and the situation for the government became untenable, pro-Russia president Viktor Yanukovych fled the country for exile in Moscow.

Two months later, President Biden—again, the White House's go-to guy on foreign policy—met with Devon Archer at the White House.

Just days later, in what the Bidens would later assure us was a crazy coincidence, Devon Archer joined the board of Burisma Holdings, an energy company owned by a corrupt Ukrainian oligarch named Mykola Zlochevsky. Six days later, according to a report prepared by the Senate Committee on Homeland Security and Governmental affairs, "British officials seized $23 million from the London bank accounts of . . . Zlochevsky."[11]

Fourteen days later, Hunter Biden joined the board of Burisma.

Years later, when the contents of Hunter Biden's laptop became public, the American people would learn the terms of this strange agreement. I don't mean the official terms, which were made public almost immediately. Even then, it was public knowledge Hunter was being paid the absurd sum of $80,000 per month to attend a few board meetings and conferences, despite no experience in the energy sector whatsoever. (Cocaine benders apparently do not count as experience in the energy world.)

What the public *didn't* know was that shortly after he joined Burisma's board, Hunter was encouraged to arrange for "highly-recognized and influential US policy makers" to travel to Ukraine and show their support. The visits, according to Vadym Pozharskyi, another Burisma board member, were necessary to "close down any pursuits against the head of the firm."

A few months after Hunter's appointment, Joe Biden took another trip to Ukraine. During that trip, he met with Ukrainian officials and persuaded them to fire prosecutor general Viktor Shokin, who happened to be the lead investigator into corruption in Ukraine—the very corruption in which his son (and he, considering how much money "Pop" demanded from Hunter over the years), was now a willing participant.

Proudly, Joe Biden tells the story himself. Imagine being so demented—or so clueless—that you can tell this story and believe you come out looking like the good guy. In a woke world, I guess you can.

> I remember going over, convincing our team—others—that we should be providing for loan guarantees. And I went over, try to guess the 12th, 13th time to Kyiv, and . . . I was supposed to announce there was going to be another billion-dollar loan guarantee. I had gotten a commitment . . . from Poroshenko and Yatsenhuk that they would take action against the state prosecutor and they didn't. . . . And I said, "We're not going to give you the billion dollars." They said, "You have no authority. You're not the president." . . . I said, "Call him." I said, "I'm telling you, you're not getting the billion dollars." I said, "You're not getting the billion. . . . I'm leaving here in six hours. If the prosecutor is not fired, you're not getting the money." Well, son of a bitch! He got fired.[12]

With that visit over, Hunter had held up his end of the bargain. Ukraine's top prosecutor was gone, and his new employers would be allowed to keep up their corruption unabated.

Given that his official duties for Burisma amounted to little more than sitting around, cashing checks, and looking creepy, Hunter had lots of free time on his hands—and as usual, he had no trouble at all filling it up with crack, women, and, well, more crack. For months, Hunter went on drug-fueled sex binges in foreign hotels and running up his credit card bills. Judging by the videos on his laptop from this period, Hunter was just about permanently intoxicated at this time. It's hard to believe he was doing anything to earn his paychecks from Burisma . . . until you realize he didn't have to. He'd already earned his money. But just in case, Joe Biden decided to make a final visit to Ukraine four days before he was to leave office. Why did he return to Ukraine on July 16, 2017, where he is shown shaking hands with President Petro Poroshenko? Were there final additions needed to be added to their agreement? Why did Joe feel it necessary four days before he was to leave office as vice president to have an in-person meeting with the president of Ukraine—the same place he continues to send hundreds of millions of dollars as president of the United States?

In May of 2015, Hunter's brother Beau succumbed to brain cancer, leaving behind a wife, Hallie, and two children. At the funeral, Hunter spoke on the same bill as his father and President Barack Obama. He seemed to speak directly from the heart, talking about how Beau would also be defined "by the quality of his character." At times, he spoke directly to his late brother's children and his grieving widow.

Then he did something that was low even by his seemingly bottomless standards. No more than a few weeks after the funeral, Hunter Biden openly began a torrid affair with Hallie, a woman who'd just lost her husband. And I don't mean the kind of affair that involves a few dinners, expensive gifts, and the occasional extramarital dalliance. I mean Hunter Biden—whose wife, Kathleen, had been dealing with his nonsense for years—bringing his dead brother's wife down to his level, giving her drugs and filming them having sex, then posting the videos to his Pornhub account.

In 2015, after making sure Joe Biden wasn't running for president again, Hunter's wife, Kathleen, filed for divorce. From there, the relationship between Hunter and Hallie grew sour. They fought and lashed out at one another. Hunter often attacked her through her young children. The family looked on in horror. In one family group chat that included Joe and Jill Biden, Hunter's half-sister Ashley confronted Hallie about the affair, writing, "This isn't love, this is my brother high."[13]

Back in Washington, D.C., Hunter was living with Bicycles, the homeless crack dealer he'd befriended in college. She taught him how to use some of the more sophisticated crack paraphernalia, and together they smoked "a ton of crack." Hunter tried going to rehab again, but it didn't take. He also began a sexual relationship with Hallie's sister Liz, whose rent he began paying. Then, along with these considerable expenses—including $57,000 for Hallie to go to rehab in Malibu in 2017—came a blow from overseas: Burisma cut Hunter's compensation in half, leaving him with only about $500,000 per year to spend on drugs, women, and whatever expenses his father needed paid.

Which, now that he was no longer vice president, was quite a bit.

Ten Percent for the Big Guy

Say what you want about Hunter Biden, but he does have his strengths.

Multitasking, for instance.

There aren't many degenerate drug addicts in the world who can cook crack, smoke it, perform lewd sex acts while on it, *and* film the whole thing on an iPhone at the same time. That takes talent.

Which is why it comes as no surprise that even amid all these personal troubles, Hunter was still able to cook up shady overseas business deals with his Uncle Jim. In the weeks leading up to the 2020 election, one of these deals would become famous all over the country, all while the intelligence agencies and Big Tech did everything in their power to stop that from happening.

The deal began on the night of May 2, 2017, when Hunter and Jim Biden sat in the lobby of the Beverly Hilton Hotel waiting for Joe to show up. Less than four months removed from the White House, the former vice president was in Los Angeles to speak at the Milken Institute Global Conference. It seemed that Joe, who for decades had bragged about being the poorest member of Congress, was finally beginning to let his guard down; he was about to show an outsider just how involved he had always been in the business deals of Biden, Inc.

That outsider was Tony Bobulinski, a nuclear engineer and Navy veteran who'd been captain of the wrestling team at Penn State University. By the time he met the Bidens in Beverly Hills, Bobulinski had learned a great deal about Chinese finance. According to Miranda Devine of the *New York Post*, Bobulinski was "conscious that he was being vetted for a trusted role orchestrating the Biden family's existing joint venture with Chinese energy conglomerate CEFC."[14]

For Hunter Biden, the work for CEFC was immensely important. His expenses were piling up, and most of his money was gone ($500,000 per year can buy a lot of crack, but not *infinite* crack). Fortunately for him, the Chinese conglomerate, led by a man named Ye Jianming, had plenty of money, and they were willing to pay Hunter handsomely for his usual minimal efforts. According to the terms of their deal, reached just as Hunter's father had left the Naval Observatory, Hunter would be paid $10 million per year (for a minimum of three years) for "introductions alone," with some additional perks.

Given the corporate structure of CEFC, this arrangement shouldn't have been surprising. The company was able to spend so much money to buy American influence—effectively acting like a small government—because for all intents and purposes, they *were* the Chinese government. According to *National Review*, the company "aligned itself so closely with the Chinese government that it was often hard to distinguish between the two."[15]

Biden, Inc. was about to do another deal with the Chinese Communist Party. And this time, there'd be hard proof that Joe Biden—the future president of the United States, in charge of America's response to Chinese aggression—was involved in the arrangement and stood to profit from it.

When the vice president arrived at the Beverly Hilton, according to Bobulinski's account, he was tired. They spoke only for a few minutes, during which Joe thanked him for his service to the country and for "helping my son." Near the end of the conversation, Biden said he "trusted" Bobulinski, then offered to meet him again the next morning.

According to Miranda Devine, this signaled that "Bobulinski had passed the test. It was a crucial meeting, because for the first time, an outsider would see the extent to which Joe was involved in Hunter and Jim's international business. Joe was the final decision-maker. Nothing important was done without his agreement."[16]

The next day, Bobulinski watched Joe Biden give his speech, then drove across town to meet again with Jim Biden. During this second meeting, Bobulinski learned all about what the Bidens had been doing over the years to help the Chinese Communist Party achieve their goals. According to Miranda Devine, when Bobulinski asked how they were going to get away with such a criminal scheme, Jim replied, "Plausible deniability."[17] That term, originally coined during the Kennedy administration, describes the practice of keeping the president or another authority figure uninformed about illegal or underhanded activities so he can plausibly deny knowing anything if the matter becomes public.

For Bobulinski, that assurance was apparently enough for him. In the coming days, "Bobulinski incorporated SinoHawk Holdings LLC, having decided against Hunter's suggestion that they call it CEFC America." In an email sent by a representative of the group, we can see exactly who owned shares in that company, which would soon bring in piles of money from the Communist government of China:

"The equity will be distributed as follows," the email read.

20 H [Hunter]
20 RW [Rob Walker]
20 JG [James Gilliar]
20 TB [Bobulinski]
10 Jim [Biden]
10 held by H for the big guy.[18]

"The big guy?" Who could that be? You know, of course. It was none other than Joe Biden.

Around the same time, Hunter met Ye Jianming in a hotel in Miami, where they discussed business. After the dinner, Ye sent a 2.8-carat diamond to Hunter's hotel room—one of the many "perks" he would get for representing the interests of this corrupt Chinese company in the United States.

But as Hunter would soon learn, the Chinese also expected more from him. By pushing the deal with CEFC to alleviate his financial woes, Hunter had tied up the Biden family with the Chinese Communist Party in more ways than he'd realized. He was about to learn that the fun, James-Bond lifestyle that he and Devon Archer wanted to live comes with a price.

Falling Dominoes

In the summer of 2017, shortly after beginning negotiations to help CEFC invest in natural gas projects in Louisiana, Hunter Biden got a message from Ye Jianming about one of his business associates—a man named Patrick Ho. For months, federal investigators had been looking into Ho's finances, and Jianming believed they were close to finding evidence of wrongdoing.

With almost no convincing, Hunter agreed to serve as Ho's lawyer.

A few months later, in November, Ho was arrested at John F. Kennedy Airport in New York City on charges of bribery and money-laundering. His first call was to Jim Biden, who agreed to set him up with another lawyer with more experience in criminal law.

Four months after that, Ye Jianming vanished, having been detained by the Chinese government "for questioning," an ominous phrase for anyone familiar with Chinese politics. In time, investigations would reveal that Ye Jianming had used a nonprofit organization to funnel millions of dollars in bribes to several leaders in Africa. In an interview with the *New Yorker,* Hunter Biden would chalk this all up to "bad luck."[19]

But as it turned out, Hunter's bad luck was just beginning.

In June of 2018, Devon Archer was convicted of securities fraud and conspiracy to commit securities fraud for defrauding investors in sham Native American tribal bonds. In March of 2019, Patrick Ho was sentenced to three years in prison for bribery and money-laundering offenses, having executed a multi-year, multimillion-dollar scheme to bribe officials in both Chad and Uganda in order to boost CEFC.

Now, according to the Bidens, Joe did not know anything about any of these shady side deals. He didn't know that Hunter was involved with these two criminals, or even that they were criminals in the first place. But the messages contained on Hunter Biden's laptop—the ones that Big Tech and the intelligence community went to great lengths to keep from coming out before the election—directly refute this claim.

In December of 2018, shortly after the *New York Times* published an exposé on Hunter's ties to these two Chinese criminals, Joe Biden called his son. But Hunter didn't answer. Rather than following family protocol and avoiding any discussions of Biden Inc.'s crooked dealings over the phone, Joe let Hunter know that he'd read the article. Near the end of the voicemail, he let slip a line that reveals just how closely he was following the case.

"I thought the article released online," he said, "it's going to be printed tomorrow in the *Times,* was good. I think you're clear."

Although the *Times* might have been willing to give Hunter a pass, other agencies were not so quick to overlook his blatant disregard for the law. In 2018, the Justice Department opened an investigation into Hunter's overseas business deals.

Of course, before this investigation could be completed, Joe Biden surprised the world by winning the presidency, thanks to willfully silent newsrooms, some censors at Twitter and Facebook who had been previously warned by the FBI to be on the lookout for Russian disinformation in the form of a laptop, and fifty-one intelligence officers whose political affiliations were more important to their oath of sovereignty.

Hunter is one of the final dominoes left to fall to fully expose the Biden Crime Syndicate. Few people have fully reviewed the contents of Hunter Biden's laptop, but it appears there was nothing in the world of Hunter and Jim Biden that "the big guy" didn't sign off on. When Joe talks tough to Vladimir Putin over his invasion of Ukraine, one has to wonder (since his son received millions from both Russia and Ukraine) if he means anything of what he says. When he's letting Beijing siphon off the oil from our strategic petroleum reserve, he does so knowing his son's involvement with CEFC China Energy. In fact, Hunter and James Biden had an arrangement where the Chinese Communist Government connected CEFC funneled $5 million to Hunter and James Biden to compensate them for work done while Joe Biden was vice president. When Joe insists on the United States transitioning to green energy, he knows full well we need to purchase lithium batteries from China.

If you had any doubt that Joe Biden is corrupt, consider this. As we go to print, more and more classified documents are being found at his home and business office in varying locations. Some of these documents were removed when Joe was a senator. In order for him as a senator to even see classified documents, he would have to have gone into a SCIF (sensitive compartmented information facility) and he would not be allowed to remove those items. We now know that he did, illegally. You may recall Sandy Berger was prosecuted for stuffing classified documents in his socks. Joe also took documents that were classified when he was vice president. All these documents are six to ten years old. We know some involved classified information about Ukraine. We also know that Hunter Biden was living in the home—paying rent to his father for a house whose monthly rent should have been no more than seven thousand a month. Was Hunter Biden funneling money from China to his dad? Were the documents that we now know are in the same house that Hunter was living in and paying that rent for one year accessible to him? The answer is an unqualified yes. The documents were found in a garage right next to Joe's shiny Corvette.

By now you should think that Joe Biden is corrupt. But as strange as it sounds, that's the *least* of his problems. It's now about us. Have Hunter's business dealings affected Joe's decisions from the White House? It's now a pressing question. America's commitment to Ukraine has become America's biggest voluntary expenditure since the invasion of Iraq. The oligarchs' overtures to the Biden clan have become one of the biggest heists in history. As of this writing, at Biden's urging, Congress has approved $113 billion in aid to Ukraine.[20] Most Americans don't realize that this aid goes far above just supplying the country weapons or training or military intelligence. It also involves simply sending the country eye-watering amounts of cash. Roughly a third of U.S. aid has been purely economic in nature. More than $10 billion has been spent simply propping up the Ukrainian government by paying the salaries of its employees . . . *if* that's what it's actually being used for. According to a published cable from America's own ambassador in Kyiv, when it comes to tracing how America's money is distributed, "standard verification measures are sometimes impracticable or impossible."[21] For ordinary Ukrainians, Russia's invasion and the ongoing war are the worst calamity to befall their country since World War II. But for connected oligarchs, it is a bonanza of unprecedented scale.

So where else might Americans be caught between the Bidens' financial interest and their obligations to other countries? Could there be any with China? Is the $1.7 trillion omnibus bill that Joe Biden signed on December 28, 2022, more about business with China than the needs of ordinary Americans? The green energy piece of that omnibus bill with historic funding for clean energy benefits

China in their manufacturing of lithium batteries for the mandatory (in some states) electric cars.

Could there be even more corruption, unhidden, that wasn't logged on Hunter's laptop? Could there be conversations and meetings that happened long ago, and need a serious investigation before they will come to light? It's possible. In a letter to the Department of Justice, Senator Chuck Grassley raised a disturbing possibility that, so far, has not been adequately investigated: What if Hunter's massive CEFC payoff wasn't payment for future services, but compensation for past ones, delayed until Joe Biden was no longer vice president?

In the pay-to-play world of the Biden family, anything is possible.

Crossing the Blue Line

Among the many insane left-wing narratives that took hold during the Obama years, one stood out above the rest: that the United States of America, particularly when it came to policing, was an evil, racist place to live—one that was not only unpleasant for African Americans, but dangerous, even lethal for them.

It was a lie. In fact, if anything deserves to be called "The Big Lie" in American politics, it's that.

But thanks to the Radical Left, it became one of the fastest-spreading lies in world history.

Unfounded Accusations

One of the consequences of social media has been the birth of the viral, amateur video. The disputes, confrontations, and meltdowns that previously only existed in the memories of direct observers now live forever online. And while videos can illuminate, they can also deceive.

Since the beginning of the Obama administration, leftists have created an entire genre of viral video clips of unarmed black men being shot or killed by police. The Twitterati have encouraged their followers to believe that sad incidents like this happen all the time, and that those caught on video are just a tiny minority of what is actually an epidemic. As a prosecutor I have long believed that crimes are not defined by color but by actions. For me, it was always about right and wrong. As district attorney, I prosecuted and con- victed a white New York City police officer for shooting a black man over a parking space. Little did I know, until I was visited by several black reverends that it was the first such murder conviction in New York state history. For millions of well-intentioned people, these Twitter videos—and the never-ending streams of commentary about them—were proof there really *was* some epidemic of police violence in the United States, and that it was aimed squarely at unarmed blacks. Why? Nothing more or less than widespread police racism and white supremacy.

You know the names: Michael Brown. Eric Garner. Trayvon Martin. Breonna Taylor. George Floyd. When the right story arrived, with the right images and sufficiently damning (or at least unclear) fact pattern, TV networks gave the killing wall-to-wall coverage, while press outlets gave moral cover for angry protests and even full- blown riots.

These deaths were a classic example of the press's power to shape narratives. Watch a steady diet of CNN, and one comes away with the impression that police killings are common, and that those killed are almost exclusively black and unarmed.

In February of 2021, a poll asked Americans across the political spectrum to estimate how many unarmed African American men they believed were killed by police in the United States in the year

2019. Remember that this poll took place less than one year after a summer of rioting and looting, largely organized and encouraged on social media, during which several prominent Democrats declared that the "epidemic" of police violence against black men needed to stop.

According to the poll, 37 percent of people who identify as "liberal" believed that at least 1,000 unarmed black men were killed by police in the year 2019. Among people who considered themselves "very liberal," that number was 52 percent. In fact, more than 20 percent of people who identified as "very liberal" believed that at least *ten thousand* unarmed African American men were killed by police every year.[1]

So, what was the real number? Well, according to the *Washington Post*'s own police shootings database, in 2019, the total number of unarmed black men shot dead by police was . . . eleven.[2]

Not eleven *hundred*. Eleven. Ten and add one. The same number of men on one side of a football game.

People weren't just mistaken and misguided. They were misguided by orders of magnitude. It was a mistake so enormous, that it simply was not possible without a malicious and highly successful disinformation campaign. Imagine how alarmed we might be if people who identified as "very liberal," when asked how many days were in a week, responded with "at least 7,000." Imagine what we would think if a considerable number of "very liberal" people believed that the average American consumed somewhere around 3,000 meals a day, or that the number of past U.S. presidents was somewhere in the neighborhood of 45,000. *That* is the kind of disinformation we are talking about. And it's not an accident. It's deliberate.

In real life, the pattern of police killings is nothing like the hysteria presented to the American public on cable news or in the pages of our largest newspapers. In 2021, American police shot and killed 1,047 people, according to the *Washington Post*'s database. Of those, the *Post* was able to determine the race of 840. Of those, the number shot and killed who were black was 233. The number of white people shot and killed? 446. The number of unarmed people (of any race) shot and killed was just 32. The number of unarmed blacks? Just like in 2019, there were only 11.[3]

When American police use force, it is overwhelmingly against armed criminals who pose an imminent danger. And even when police do use excessive force on an innocent person, they do so against all races.

I'm sure, for instance, that most Americans have never heard the story of Tony Timpa of Dallas, Texas. Timpa was a schizophrenic who called the police on himself, telling the 911 dispatcher that he was depressed and had not taken his medication. By the time Dallas police arrived, Timpa had already been handcuffed by security guards. Nevertheless, the police forced Timpa to the ground and held him there, pressing a knee to his back as he squirmed and cried for his mother. Eventually, Timpa lost consciousness, but instead of giving first aid, officers joked about later waking him in time for school.

Timpa never woke up. An autopsy determined that he died within minutes of officers' arrival, from a combination of cocaine in his system and the physical restraints of the officers.

In even its smallest details, Timpa's story is uncannily close to another story you know all about: the death of George Floyd. But while "Floyd" is one of the most famous names and faces in history, Timpa is forgotten. His story never made national news. It barely made the *local* news. There were no protests, no rallies, and no riots for Tony Timpa. Why? You can guess: Tony was just a white thirty-two-year-old. He didn't fit the narrative.

A small group of left-wing activists has managed to convince the entire country that there was an epidemic of racist violence based on little-to-no evidence, relying completely on viral photos and videos of a few isolated incidents—and even in those isolated incidents, the evidence was often anything but conclusive. "Hands up, don't shoot" was popularized as, supposedly, the last words of Ferguson teenager Michael Brown. But a thorough investigation by the Department of Justice under Obama's wingman Eric Holder determined that the "hands up, don't shoot" narrative was a lie: Brown never put his hands up, never attempted to surrender to Officer Darren Wilson, and was shot dead while charging him to attack.

America has been mentally warped by an extremely successful propaganda campaign. In many ways, it was the first shot fired in the Left's Takedown of America.

This Big Lie of the Left would be wicked even if its only effect was to tar the character of America's hardworking police officers of all races. But it did far worse than that. When the Radical Left launched into Black Lives Matter mode during Obama's presidency, it destroyed decades of progress on race relations in the United States. In his book *The War on the West*, Douglas Murray summed up the grim evidence:

> Polls showed that positive views on the state of race relations in America peaked at the time of President Obama's inauguration in 2009. At that time, a CBS/New York Times poll found that 66 percent of Americans thought that race relations were generally good. But as it tracked the polls over the following years, the Associated Press noted that views on race "started to sour" in 2014. One interpretation of this is that America became more racist over the two terms of

its first black president. Another is that the media attention on certain incidents—whether justifiable or not—helped to alter America's view of itself.[4]

For decades, Americans had generally been optimistic about race relations in their country. From the civil rights movement of the '50s and '60s onward, there was a powerful sense of progress and improvement in America's goal of becoming a country where "all men are created equal." Jim Crow vanished. Segregation ended. Opportunity gaps closed. Americans of all races thought that things were going pretty well. But then, around the year 2014, something shifted, almost overnight. In 2002, 70 percent of black Americans told Gallup that black-white relations in America were very or somewhat good. By 2020, that number was down to 36 percent. And just like in the CBS/NYT poll mentioned above, the key turning point was in the second half of Obama's presidency. Something happened around the year 2014 that made a majority of Americans rethink whether their country was getting less racist every day—something they believed just a few years earlier. Looking back, it is clear that that "something" was a coordinated campaign, begun on social media and dragged into the newsrooms of America by the Radical Left, to deliberately sow the seeds of division among black and white people in the United States of America. It was a campaign based on lies, with core tenets that were easily disprovable. But thanks to a chilling atmosphere in which anyone who raised questions about the movement was swiftly silenced and called out as a racist, the lies spread, and the campaign was successful.

Consider what happened to the few brave people who tried to stand up and tell the truth, many of them people initially sympathetic to the Left's cause. When the conservative writer Andrew

Sullivan attempted to publish a column in *New York* magazine that referred to the widespread riots that occurred during the summer of 2020 as *riots* instead of peaceful protests, the left-wing staff staged their own internal riot and got him fired.

Two years later Zac Kriegman, a data scientist at Thomson Reuters, one of the top news agencies in the world, sent a memo that challenged the Radical Left's prevailing narrative on race. Kriegman had worked at Thomson Reuters for six years; during that time, he had developed a reputation for scrupulous adherence to the facts and a willingness to follow important stories to their sources. That's how he worked his way up to the position of Director of Data Science, which came with a salary of $350,000. Obviously, this company—which reached an audience of one billion people worldwide, including almost all top law firms in the United States—trusted him and his judgment. That is, until he went against the party line on racism.

According to an account that he wrote afterward, Kriegman had noticed that employees at Reuters were using the company's "internal collaboration platform, the Hub . . . to post about 'the self-indulgent tears of white women' and the danger of 'white privilege glasses.' They'd share articles with titles like 'Seeing White,' 'Habits of Whiteness" and 'How to Be a Better White Person.' There was fervent and vocal support for Black Lives Matter at every level of the company. No one challenged the racial essentialism or the groupthink."[5]

Instead of mindlessly following along, Kriegman decided to put his expertise in action, and looked at the data. What he found shocked him. As it turned out, if you looked at the numbers—*really* looked at them, in a way that only a trained data scientist can—almost every piece of the Black Lives Matter platform came crashing down. Citing the work of Roland Freyer and other researchers,

Kriegman concluded that, after adjusting for other factors, American blacks actually were *not* more likely to be shot than other races. In fact, he said, if anything they were "slightly *less likely* to be shot."

After compiling all his research, Kriegman wrote a long, detailed memo and posted it to the employee portal. This memo attempted to refute the narratives that BLM was pushing, and included the striking statistic: "On an average year, 18 unarmed black people and 26 unarmed white people are shot by police. By contrast, roughly 10,000 black people are murdered by criminals in their own neighborhoods."[6]

From the moment the post went up, the knives were out. Fellow employees deemed the study an exercise in "whitesplaining." Others said it was "laughable" and refused to engage with it. In June, Kriegman was fired—not for any shortcoming in his job performance, but because he had dared to go against the sacred religion of wokeness in the workplace.

Every few days, it seems, a similar incident happens somewhere in America. It happens often that ordinary Americans have learned there is a cost of speaking out against the Left, whether it's at school, at work, and sometimes even at the dinner table. This climate of fear allowed the Black Lives Matter narrative to spread without pushback or criticism.

During the same period that Kriegman was going through his ordeal, Reuters posted numerous stories pushing the BLM line with information that was biased and often outright false. In one story, they reported that black Americans are "more likely to be killed by police" despite the facts saying the opposite. In another story Reuters published just as the George Floyd riots were beginning, they referred to "a wave of killings of African-Americans by police using unjustified lethal force." This "wave" never existed, except in the heads of

Reuters' reporters, editors, and their colleagues at America's other narrative-setting news outlets.

These stories were far greater lies than anything ever written about Hunter Biden. But they were never flagged as "misinformation" by the regime. The people in charge decided that these lies were permissible, because they served a good cause—stoking hatred against America's police, one of the essential pillars in an orderly society.

So how did this lie affect the very people that the Radical Left said they were trying to help? Let's take a look.

The Takedown of Police

They will deny it now, but during the George Floyd Riots that occurred in the summer of 2020, the Radical Left told us *exactly* what they wanted. Every mainstream media network in the country was cheering them on. So was every Fortune 500 company. Every Democrat was on board, and more than a few terrified Republicans. They were looting stores, torching cars, and even burning down an entire police precinct, and still getting praised as "mostly peaceful." They felt unstoppable and almost all-powerful. They felt strong enough to say what their *real* agenda was, without any dissembling or deflection.

And what they wanted, they said, was to "abolish the police." A self-described "organizer against criminalization" named Mariame Kaba laid all the Left's cards on the table in a June 2020 op-ed for the *New York Times*: "Yes, We Mean Literally Abolish the Police."

"A 'safe' world is not one in which the police keep black and other marginalized people in check through threats of arrest, incarceration, violence and death," Kaba wrote in her piece. Municipal police forces, she said, only exist to "[suppress] marginalized populations to protect the status quo." Then, Kaba got to the "ransom note" portion of her essay.

"Cut the number of police in half and cut their budget in half," she wrote. "Fewer police officers equals fewer opportunities for them to brutalize and kill people. The idea is gaining traction in Minneapolis, Dallas, Los Angeles, and other cities."[7]

You bet it was.

In Minneapolis, Radical Left activists exploited George Floyd's death by demanding the city's police force be completely dismantled. In its place, they suggested, the city create a new "public safety agency." According to the activists behind this ballot initiative, getting rid of the whole department was the only way to stop police officers from "brutalizing" communities of color. In an incredible display of lunacy, the Minneapolis City Council's thirteen members voted *unanimously* to ask the city's voters whether they wanted to amend the city charter and allow the abolition of all police. Fortunately, 56 percent of voters in Minneapolis saw through this and voted against the ballot initiative . . . but 44 percent actually voted to support it.[8]

In the end, activists never managed to abolish the Minneapolis Police Department. But they did manage to destroy businesses, homes, and property and create a blight on a city that will take a generation to repair. Yet, even ignoring everything they stole from the city's Targets, they didn't go home empty-handed. In December of 2020, they got the city government to divert about $8 million from the proposed police budget to other city services. In the admiring words of the *New York Times*, the small monetary shift had the potential of "transforming public safety in a city where law enforcement has long been accused of racism."[9]

That was more than two years ago. So how have things gone?

Well, in 2019, Minneapolis had 48 homicides. I
the George Floyd riots swept the city and the poli
debate raged, murders rose to 84, a 75 percent increa
year. In 2021, with the riots past and their newly "transf
lic safety arm, the city logged a staggering 96 murde
figure in twenty-five years and exactly double the mark
years prior.[10]

The mayhem in Minneapolis and the wider anti-
spread across the blue state of Minnesota causing crime
Assaults on police officers rose 35 percent from 2020
Carjackings, previously so rare the state didn't bother
them, became a twice-daily occurrence.[11]

During that time, citizens cried out for help. Many
were the very "people of color" that the left-wing poli
Minneapolis claimed they were protecting. In a poll ta
major local news organizations in September of 2021, an
75 percent of black voters said they were against cutting the
of police officers.[12]

One black community leader named Don Samue
attempted to sue the city for not keeping an adequate nui
police officers on the streets. In his many letters to the city
he described the unbelievable devastation being experienced i
munities of color during the push to defund the police. *The*
a left-wing magazine which profiled Samuels, wrote he "pai
grim picture of the neighborhood: a story about a young gi
was killed while playing on a trampoline, a teenager who was s
the neck twice, a neighbor so afraid of stray bullets that she ins
a bulletproof barrier behind her headboard."[13]

Speaking to MPR News in the fall of 2021, black Minnea
resident Ea Porter said she believed black voters were "more l

to feel the effects of the lack of effective, and inadequate policing."[14] Toward the end of the interview, Porter delivered a stirring message to the well-off, mostly white liberal activists trying to push their trendy "defund the police" nonsense on people who live in communities where crime rates are rising.

"Don't experiment on us," she said. "Because we're the ones that are going to be hit hardest first."[15]

But the great experiment wasn't just in Minneapolis, and it wasn't just in Minnesota. In the three years that have passed since the George Floyd "racial reckoning," almost every blue city in America has become a Frankenstein laboratory of anti-police, pro-crime policies, with devastating results. In Chicago, Mayor Lori Lightfoot pledged to cut $80 million from the police budget. Crime rose sharply. By December of 2021, Mayor Lightfoot was begging the FBI to help her stem the tide of murders and carjackings wracking the streets of her depopulating city.[16]

In Portland, Oregon, Mayor Ted Wheeler disbanded the city's Gun Violence Reduction Team in response to complaints that the team was, you guessed it, racist. The result: Portland went from 36 murders in 2019[17] to an all-time record of 96 in 2022.[18]

Nationwide, the American murder rate rose by close to 30 percent from 2019 to 2020, by far the biggest one-year increase in our history.[19] In 2021, the murder rate rose another 4.3 percent. In both years, the increase in slayings was concentrated in America's Democrat "progressive," lawless urban centers.

Unsurprisingly, in many of these bloodstained cities, survival-minded politicians have tried to make reversals. They've lost the talking points of the Radical Left and tried to reinvest in police forces.

But it has proven difficult to put the genie back in the bottle. In many places, emboldened criminals have simply stopped fearing

police. Even more important, police themselves have been quitting in droves, both retiring and resigning. In Minneapolis, the size of the police department shrank by a full third from 2019 to 2022, as hundreds of officers quit while only a few dozen applicants stepped forward to replace them. Who can blame them? Minneapolis police have learned that when they use force against suspects, politicians will side with criminals instead of them. They have learned that with enough public outcry over a viral video, they will be thrown to the wolves. They have learned that the absolute *best*-case scenario for their careers will still mean a life of getting accused of racism, no matter what the evidence is. And, don't forget, the job still carries all the traditional risks of being shot and killed by a criminal in the line of duty. In a stunning turn of events, Minneapolis has learned that people don't want to do a difficult, dangerous job when they will be treated as villains for even attempting it.

The Minneapolis experience continues to play out in blue cities across the country.

Things got so bad that even Biden was silent as America burned during the summer of 2020, and didn't bother to mention any of it during the Democratic National Convention for president.

Almost two years later, on March 1, 2022, in his State of the Union address Biden let the radical wing of his party know that "defund the police" was dead . . . at least for the moment. For once, he delivered his lines exactly as his speechwriters had intended.

"We should all agree," he said. "The answer is not to defund the police. It's to fund the police. Fund them. Fund them. Fund them with resources and training."[20] Finally, Biden admitted what America already knew, and that was there is no nation—no orderly society—without law and order. The sad part is that too many people suffered and died while the Left, including Biden and his half-wit vice president, ignored the violence in America. Kamala not only ignored it, she was part of the group looking to put criminals back in the streets in a bizarre cashless bail effort through the Minnesota bail fund.

Joe Biden's final admission in 2022 was not so much a change of heart as it was a recognition by Democrats that they were losing on the crime issue. The midterms were right around the corner and the polling made it clear that America was not happy with the "defund the police" movement.

In Nancy Pelosi's own city of San Francisco, the Tenderloin District became a post-apocalyptic zone where zombie-like addicts and homeless shoot up, shoot each other, or simply wait for death in the streets of what was once one of America's most beautiful cities. But by 2022, the Tenderloin calamity had become so severe that even Pelosi, who has shown an unusual willingness to keep spitting lies long after she's been proven wrong, declared the idea of defunding cops to be "dead."

But it doesn't matter if Democrats have changed their tune. As of this writing, America's murder rate is still almost one-third higher than it was before 2020's "racial reckoning" and anti-police hysteria. That means that literally thousands of people have died, and thousands more will die, who would have lived if not for the anti-police, pro-criminal rhetoric of the Left.

After Biden's 2022 State of the Union address calling to drop the "de-" from "fund the police," most news networks pretended that the "defund the police" movement had simply appeared one day out of nowhere, without any constituency. They imagined that hundreds of elected Democrats had never said anything in its favor. They pretended, in short, that Democrats had been tackling the country's exploding crime rate, just like Biden was promising.

Hogwash. Even after Biden's backtrack, the Left's dishonest and downright poisonous anti-cop sentiment continues to infect our cities and neighborhoods.

Consider another video that went viral, four months after Biden's "fund the police" pitch, in July 2022. The video, recorded by a bystander, shows two police officers standing on a corner in St. Paul, Minnesota. According to the *Daily Mail,* the officers, both black men, were on their way "to serve a search warrant in the hunt for a murder suspect." But on their way, they were stopped on the sidewalk by four children, one of whom looked no older than five.

In the video, as the officers try to speak with the children, the youngest one—dressed in nothing but underwear—screams "shut up, b*tch," and punches one of the officers in the leg. The child jumps around, putting both arms out the way adults do when they're about to begin a fist fight, yelling "shut the f**k up," while his young friends cheer him on. Eventually, the officers stop trying to win the children over and walk away.[21]

As the columnist at Alpha News who first reported on the video pointed out, this wasn't the children's fault. They were simply acting as they had been taught. Their behavior was no different from what the whole country had seen for two years in cities such as Minneapolis, Chicago, and Portland, Oregon. Since they were old enough to understand language, these children were probably bombarded with talking points about how police in the United States only exist to kill young black children. Some of this propaganda may have come from their parents. The rest would come from the television, the radio, Twitter, and most toxic of all, from teachers.

It doesn't have to be this way. Violence and hate are learned behaviors, and lies will triumph unless they are met with truth. The anti-police mania will never end unless we stop it. And that doesn't just mean funding the police. It means aggressively confronting, rejecting, and refuting the lies of BLM and its affiliated movements. American police are not serial racist murderers. I know, I spent thirty-two years working with them in police stations, DA officers, and courtrooms. In fact, America's police departments are some of the most racially integrated institutions in American life. And until they were sabotaged in 2020, they had been some of our most successful too. From 1990 through the mid-2010s, while American schools, colleges, manufacturing, and quality of life all declined, American police successfully halved the murder rate, saving tens of thousands of black lives in the process. Cities like New York and Washington D.C. became safe to walk through once again.

Thanks to BLM's insistent, repeated lies, instead of being praised for their transcendent achievement, police have become the villains . . . and the achievement is vanishing before our eyes.

"Triggered" by Taxes

While American police were treated like a criminal gang, Black Lives Matter itself was treated like a collection of the world's greatest humanitarians. As rioters burned down Minneapolis Police Third Precinct, donations poured into the Black Lives Matter organization from celebrities and corporations like Amazon, Microsoft, Airbnb, and Coca-Cola.[22]

Exactly where *did* all that money go?

If you needed any more proof that Black Lives Matter, the organization, was nothing more than a front for hucksters and charlatans, look no further than the empty checkbook they had by the end of the year 2021. Clearly, this group intended to profit from the takedown of America while it was happening, collect their "white guilt money," and then spend it while the cities of this country burned.

Given how much support they had from the media and corporate America while the riots were at their worst, they probably thought no one would notice. But eventually they got caught.

In April of 2021, the *New York Post* zeroed in on the finances of Patrisse Khan-Cullors, the co-founder of the Black Lives Matter Global Network Foundation who had often described herself as a Marxist. For years, Khan-Cullors had been making money by scamming guilt-ridden white people into buying her books and giving her high-profile television deals, which she used to "educate" them about racism. During the Obama years, business had been good. During the Trump years, business had been great. But when George Floyd breathed his last on a Minneapolis street, Khan-Cullors struck gold.

Suddenly, nearly-infinite money was pouring into BLM's coffers—about $90 million by year's end. At the time, those who sent in money believed they were helping to protect African Americans from police violence and systemic racism through grassroots activism.

What were they really paying for? Mansions, mostly.

In April of 2021, the *New York Post* exposed a real estate buying spree by the proud Marxist Patrisse: four properties adding up to a total of $3.2 million. In 2016, as BLM's profile rose in the wake of Michael Brown's death, Khan-Cullors picked up an Inglewood home for about half a million dollars. In 2018, she added a $590,000 home in South Los Angeles. In early 2020, Khan-Cullors added a 3.2-acre ranch home in Conyers, Georgia. And finally, in the spring of 2021, after BLM's huge 2020 haul, Khan-Cullors upgraded in a big way, buying a $1.4 million home on a secluded road just outside Malibu, in a (heavily-white) part of Los Angeles.[23]

But incredibly, the spending spree didn't end there. In the spring of 2021, after details about the buying binge came out, Khan-Cullors and three other Black Lives Matter founders responded with a YouTube video memorializing the first anniversary of George Floyd's death. Khan-Cullors says that she's tired of attacks on her from the "right-wing media machine," which she says have sent her into "survival mode." Her two co-founders agree, saying that all the right-wing attempts to "cancel" them had failed. In the video, the three women snack on cheese and wine in the courtyard of what looks to be an expensive home . . . but not any of the four expensive homes Khan-Cullors already owned.[24]

In spring 2022, *New York* magazine (hardly a conservative outlet) revealed the truth. In October 2020, BLM had spent $6 million cash on a sprawling 6,500-square-foot home. The house's palatial amenities included more than half a dozen bedrooms and bathrooms, a soundstage, several fireplaces, a pool, a guest house, and enough parking for more than twenty vehicles. The magazine's reporting revealed that Black Lives Matter purchased the house in secret, sending several internal emails about how to hide the massive purchase from the media. Their plan was to pretend that it was an "influencer house," to be used only for filming content. But that was another lie, and within a few weeks Khan-Cullors admitted the home had been used to throw multiple lavish parties, including her son's birthday bash. What a use of $90 million in donations for "racial justice"![25]

As scrutiny of the purchase increased, Khan-Cullors whined that the basic transparency documents required of charities were "unsafe" for black women such as her. According to the *Washington Examiner*, which covered an event where she spoke:

"It is such a trip now to hear the term '990,'" Cullors said Friday during an event at the Vashon Center for the Arts. "I'm, like, ugh. It's, like, triggering."

. . . Cullors said activists suffer trauma and that their lives are put at risk when charities under their control are required to disclose publicly what they did with their tax-deductible donations.

"This doesn't seem safe for us, this 990 structure—this nonprofit system structure," Cullors said. "This is, like, deeply unsafe. This is being literally weaponized against us, against the people we work with."[26]

Well, Patrice, we're *all* triggered when it comes to taxes. But we follow the law. The woman who had spearheaded the mass defamation of nearly a million police officers however felt no need to obey the rules herself.

Recent disclosures have shown that rather than using all their money to help struggling communities, the founders of Black Lives Matter have "spread the wealth" all over the place. One of these places was the stock market, where BLM founders spent about $32 million in stocks to "ensure that the foundation's work continues into the future." (Of course, thanks to Biden's leadership, that $32 million in stocks isn't worth so much anymore!) The same year, the founder of Black Lives Matter paid $840,000 to a company called Cullors Protection, which just so happened to be owned by her brother Paul. This money had to go to her brother, of course, because BLM doesn't trust the former police officers who typically run security firms. But that doesn't explain why another $969,000 had to go to Damon Turner, a man who fathered a child with Khan-Cullors, for "production, design and media services."[27]

And all that was just over the course of a single year. Who knows where the money has gone since.

But by this point, it didn't matter that the founders of Black Lives Matter were exposed as transparent frauds. The dangerous ideology they helped create had already spread to nearly every major institution in this country. Every day, the BLM lie continues to create a scenario of law enforcement skepticism and a loss of faith in our criminal justice system, while its creators use guilt money to finance their fraudulent lifestyle and live it up in mansions paid for by suckers who don't have the balls to ask for their money back even though they know it's been misspent.

Aiding and Abetting Violent Criminal Conduct

In early 2022, then-White House Press Secretary Jen Psaki sat for an interview on a liberal podcast called *Pod Save America.* This show, started in 2017 by three doofuses who met while working in the Obama White House, bills itself as "no-bullshit conversation about politics hosted by former Obama aides." (Probably the only time "no-bullshit" and "former Obama aides" have ever appeared in the same sentence.)

On the day of Psaki's interview, February 1, inflation was rising rapidly. Americans fretted about whether they could afford their rapidly-rising rent *and* soaring food costs, and still afford to fill their cars with $4.53/gallon gas to get to work. The White House was under siege, bombarded with questions about what they planned to do. Meanwhile, Russia had just accused the United States of "provoking escalation in Ukraine" at the United Nations. War looked (and in fact, was) imminent. There were fears it could go nuclear.

So what did Ms. Psaki want to talk about?

Me, it turns out.

Psaki answered a few questions, then turned her attention to a bank of televisions on the wall of her office, each of which was playing a different cable channel.

"So, right now," she said, "just to give you a sense . . . CNN: Pentagon: As many as 8,500 troops on heightened alert.' Okay, true. Same on MSNBC. CNBC is doing their own thing about the market. And then, on Fox, is Jeanine Pirro talking about 'soft-on-crime consequences.' I mean, what does that even mean?"[1]

What does it mean? I know Psaki can't be that dumb (but then again, she is a leftist!), so I'll be generous and explain. "Soft on crime" means an administration that advocates for criminals instead of victims. "Soft on crime" means sitting silently when American businesses and cities are torched by those demanding "social justice." "Soft on crime" means *whatever* America was doing from 2019 to 2021, when we sent crime soaring 42 percent in just two years.

It was the worst explosion of criminality in American history. It costs thousands of lives. And yes, whatever Little Red Lying Hood might think, it's worth talking about.

America's Crime Crisis

There was a time in our history when the victims of crime looked to frontier justice as the way to avenge the wrongs against them. Frontier justice didn't come from police or courts or judges. Mostly, it was meted out by one's kin. Women and children were dependent on their fathers, husbands, and brothers to protect them. Frontier justice was ad-hoc, inconsistent, and shockingly violent.

Today, as part of living in a civilized society, we reject this old vigilante way of doing things. Instead of taking the law into our own hands, we all surrender this power to the government, which in turn promises to protect us and punish criminals on our behalf. This is the social contract we have forged. It is the single most important responsibility we expect government to meet.

But today's left-wing governments are not meeting it. Instead of protecting victims, they have taken the side of criminals, with disastrous consequences. In the last three years we have seen countless businesses destroyed, burnt down, and demolished under the guise of "social justice." The people who have suffered most are not being compensated, or even heard.

The people who brought us the sham of "white privilege" are now creating a new, terrifying, and very real system of "criminal privilege." The criminal justice system is turned on its head. Society is recast as the perpetrator, the criminal as a victim, and the *actual* victim becomes mere collateral damage.

For years I have questioned even the term "criminal justice system." It ought to be called the "victim justice system." The victim who is targeted for no good reason, who suffered greatly and will never be made whole again. The victim who never asked to be a part of any system. Criminals choose to victimize. Victims don't choose to be violated.

Yet to look at our system you might think it's the opposite, that criminals are the ones who have had their lives damaged, and who must be made whole. Every part of the system functions to allow the criminal free rein as quickly as possible. When they commit crimes, they are rarely arrested. When they are arrested, they are routinely released without bail. When they are convicted, they rarely receive harsh sentences. And when given harsh sentences, the Left immediately begins to work, relentlessly, to win them clemency. This is the heart of "criminal privilege."

Bailed Out

One of the first signs of growing "criminal privilege" in our system, a canary in the coal mine of our failing law and order system, was the concept of "cashless bail."

The concept of bail is enshrined explicitly in the text of our Bill of Rights, in the Eighth Amendment: "*Excessive bail shall not be required*, nor excessive fines imposed, nor cruel and unusual punishments inflicted." And so it was, for more than two hundred years. Judges sized up a criminal offender, weighed their character, criminal record, employment, danger to the public, and more, and used it to make an assessment about their likelihood of returning to court to face charges, and their odds of offending again if let back onto the streets. Then, the judge would impose a fee on the offender. If the offender paid the fee, and later appeared in court, that fee would be returned. If he didn't, it would be forfeited. And if the defendant was simply too dangerous to be let out at all, no bail would be granted.

The system I described above should sound familiar to you. It's how the system has worked all our lives. It's how the system probably does still work for many of you, and lo and behold, you likely live in a place that is safer than a liberal city.

But in the Left's urban bastions of insanity, a very different concept of bail has come into being. To hear them talk about it, you would think that bail was unconstitutional rather than a literal clause of the Constitution.

And so, across the country, Radical Left activists have tried to replace traditional bail with "cashless bail." On the grounds that cash bail discriminates against the poor, they are passing laws where huge numbers of criminals are either held indefinitely until trial, or else released with only a promise to eventually show up for a court hearing.

In practice, what "cashless bail" has meant is immediately releasing thousands of antisocial habitual criminals onto the streets to commit more crimes—sometimes even multiple crimes on the same day.

We've seen this outcome in New York, which in 2019 passed a sweeping "bail reform" law. From 2019 to 2022, the number of criminals with three or more arrests for robbery, burglary, or larceny in a single year rose nearly 26 percent. The number of serial shoplifters rose more than a third. Since that bill has passed, a group of just ten career criminals has racked up nearly *five hundred* arrests.[2]

In October 2022, NYPD officers arrested Clarence Anderson for shoving a stranger onto the subway tracks, and attacking another complete stranger with a rock on the same day. Anderson could have easily killed either person, but the attacks would have never happened at all if he had simply been kept behind bars after any of his *forty-five* preceding arrests.[3]

On May 11, 2022, New York attorney general Letitia James said the state's crime spike (which would become the number one issue for New York voters in the midterms), "didn't warrant changes" to the cashless bail law. Speaking to Jim Owles Liberal Democratic LGBT Club—because, you know, it had been thirty seconds since she pandered to the extreme left—James said we should:

> . . . follow the data and really look at it from an analytical perspective. That means ensuring we are resisting the urge to overreact to spikes in crime that have occurred during this

pandemic, without dismantling them outright. The challenge we have faced is getting accurate and complete data. The state Office of Court Administration released data at the end of December and had to immediately revise those numbers, which shows that we don't yet have all of the information we need to guide us to a proper decision.[4]

Please.

You know where this woman could have gotten some data? Right on the front page of the next morning's *New York Post*.

There, it was reported that a police officer named Dennis Vargas was shot by a career criminal in the Bronx. The man who shot him, Rameek Smith, was arrested for gun possession two years earlier, but he was allowed to roam free under the state's bail laws even after he pled guilty to the gun charge. He was released even though he had *nine* prior charges, including, in the words of the *Post*, "a 2016 robbery that brought him probation." Luckily, things went right in the days after Officer Vargas was shot. He survived his wounds. In the year 2021 alone, 73 officers were murdered in the line of duty nationwide, a 63 percent rise from the year before.[5]

And it's not only police officers. When liberals allow violent criminals to walk free, we're all in danger. Take the case of Sergeant Hason Correa, a young man who survived deployment in Afghanistan only to be murdered in New York City in 2018. Correa was walking down the street when "four men and a woman pounced on him, stabbing him to death."[6] One of the men who stabbed him had been released from jail while awaiting trial.

In the years since, Hason Correa's mother, Madeline Brame, has become one of the strongest advocates for undoing the disastrous bail policies of the Left.

"Anyone who is a victim of any crime," she said shortly after her son's death, 'from the senior citizen who gets mugged for their cellphone for $30, for the woman who comes home from work and steps into the elevator and gets raped, for the 93-year-old man who is walking down the street and gets punched in the face by someone who has 103 prior arrests, there is something wrong with this picture."[7]

Sadly, Madeline Brame was not speaking hypothetically. Each one of the people she mentioned was real, and so were the crimes committed against them. For the past four years, Brame and other victims' rights groups have been appealing to politicians to end so-called bail reform and restore some accountability to our criminal justice system.

In May of 2022, Biden traveled to New York City to meet with Mayor Eric Adams. Asked about bail reform, Biden delivered the lines that the Radical Left had written for him, saying that he thought "the negative side of bail reform is vastly overrated."[8] Easy for him to say. *He's* the one with full-time bodyguards.

But while Biden might call the whole problem "overrated," New York's own Democratic mayor can't be so delusional. The situation in New York post-bail reform has become so bad Eric Adams denounced the state's law as "insane." Democrat Governor Kathy Hochul who says the perception of crime by New Yorkers is actually worse than the crime problem itself has done nothing but talk the talk as New Yorkers continue to be assaulted on the subways, on the streets, and in their own homes . . . but I'll believe in Democrats actually learning their lesson when I see it happen.

They certainly aren't learning their lesson elsewhere. In Illinois, exploding crime rates didn't stop the state from becoming the first in the country to completely abolish all cash bail in a law that took effect at the start of 2023. As always, liberal lawmakers will feel very good about themselves, while ordinary citizens will pay the price.

Now, I'm not just some clueless interloper trashing how law enforcement does its job. I actually do know a little bit about crime and about law enforcement. As the first female elected district attorney, I was chief law enforcement officer for Westchester County, New York, a county with more people than a few U.S. states. Before winning that race, I was the first woman elected Westchester County judge, and before that I spent fifteen years in the trenches as an assistant DA. In those years, I helped start one of the first domestic violence units in the nation. I was a pioneer in aggressively prosecuting child abuse cases, during a time where many still thought it better to handle crimes within a family behind closed doors and far away from a courtroom.

The office of the district attorney is a battleground, where the fight between good and evil unfolds each day. My daily fare was murder, rape, violent felonies, and crimes so heinous that jurors would often look away, or just break down, crying as I described evidence to them. As prosecutors, we see the ugliest side of life, the pain that people go through for no reason. People guilty of nothing but trying to live their own lives are put through hellish personal nightmares. As prosecutors, we cannot take away their pain or turn back time to undo the damage, but we can be the avengers. We can see justice on their behalf.

All those years confronting crime directly as a prosecutor and judge taught me important lessons that somehow escape those who came after me. Perhaps the single most important lesson I learned is this: there is nothing more destructive to public safety and social harmony than flagrant, open crime going unpunished. Criminals are predators, and when they sense weakness and vulnerability, they exploit it. Only a thin blue line of law enforcement protects civilization from barbarism, and when that line wavers—or liberal politicians erase it—anarchy follows.

I understand that people like Jen Psaki and the *POD Save America* soyboys would rather not think about crime this way. They want to see crime as a complex social phenomenon which tragic people are pushed into by a society that has failed them. But having been on the front lines for over thirty years, I cannot sit quietly while those who know nothing about law enforcement destroy the safety and security of citizens in this nation. Many of their ideas have nothing whatsoever to do with making our community safer, protecting our children, reducing violence, or getting predators off the streets. Their goal is to protect the defendant at all costs, no matter how many times they have to be arrested, let out, and arrested again. The leftist framework simply does not work. Worse, it destroys businesses, cities, and human lives.

Let me be clear, every defendant is entitled to be vigorously defended in a court of law. Every person arrested for a crime is entitled to the presumption of innocence and the best legal representation they can get. I, however, have no interest in why the defendant did what he did. I don't care about his background or whatever sob story a non-profit wants to tell about him. When someone *chooses* to victimize another person, our job—*society's* job—is to make it so they cannot do it again. If this sounds unfair or callous or not compassionate enough, too bad. I don't lose sleep over it.

I wish I could say that every person entrusted with the job of DA shared my worldview. Sadly, it's not true.

The Soros Prosecutors

In November 2021, Milwaukee district attorney John Chisholm had to assess a case that had just come before his office. The case concerned a thirty-nine-year-old man who had been arrested for trying to run over his ex-girlfriend with an SUV outside of a gas station. At the time of the crime, the man already had another pending criminal charge for firing a gun at his nephew in summer 2020 in a dispute over a cell phone. But even that was far from his first crime. The man had a string of seven offenses dating back to 1999. Once, he had beaten a girlfriend so severely that a man in a neighboring hotel room overheard and called the police. Once, when pulled over for not wearing a seatbelt, the man had impulsively tried to drive away, forcing an officer to leap into his car and wrest away control of the wheel. Drugs, battery, resisting arrest, the rap sheet continued. The man also had reams of unpaid child support and, naturally, an outstanding arrest warrant for statutory rape for impregnating a fifteen-year-old girl in Nevada.

DA Chisholm took in the totality of the man's situation and concluded: *This man needs to be back on the streets! Society is at fault here!*

And so it was that Darrell Brooks went free, after paying a mere $1,000 in bail. Two days later, Brooks drove an SUV—the same SUV he used against his ex-girlfriend days earlier—through a Christmas parade crowd in Waukesha, Wisconsin. He steered from side to side with the goal of striking as many marchers and spectators as possible. At one point, Brooks leaned his head out the window because of the bodies piling up on his windshield. By the time his rampage ended, Brooks had murdered six and injured more than sixty. One of the dead was an eight-year-old boy, Jackson Sparks, whose brother Tucker survived with severe injuries. The Sparks family will never be the same. Neither will the other family and friends of Brooks' many other victims.

By the time Brooks carried out his terrorist attack, there had already been four separate incidents where Brooks, given his violent history, should have been remanded to the county jail and held until trial. But Chisholm wasn't enforcing that part of the law. His office had a higher priority: Protecting criminals from consequences, and feeling good about themselves in the process.

In the aftermath of the attack, Chisholm admitted that the $1,000 bail that his office set for Darrell Brooks was "inappropriately low."[9] But his apology made it sound like one of his assistant DA's had made a mistake, missed a comma somewhere that shifted the office's handling of Brooks from "lock up forever" to "set free immediately." Nothing of the sort happened, of course. Brooks was just one predator among many to benefit from Chisholm's policy of criminal privilege.

Brooks's horrifying case was just one of many where Chisholm's office set preposterously low bail for dangerous criminals who shouldn't have been let out at all.

So why was a pro-crime DA letting homicidal maniacs back onto the streets of Greater Milwaukee? How did Milwaukee County voters end up electing a pro-crime DA to "protect" them?

Simple: Chisholm was the product of a calculated, years-long plan to gut America's cities by infiltrating the highest levels of the criminal justice system with ideological actors who would instinctively put the criminal first and the victim last.

As a former DA myself, I know better than anyone just how important the job is, and how much damage can be done by someone who doesn't understand the job—or, in the case of the modern Left, by someone who wants to intentionally sabotage the system.

Most of the time, achieving dramatic change through politics is tough. Running for president or governor is costly, and there are countless contenders. A member of the House or Senate is just one voting member among hundreds, and their individual ability to shape legislation is limited. But for somebody plotting a takedown of America, there may be no better return on investment than a district attorney race. These races get far less funding and attention than most, and election day is often not even in November, ensuring lower voter turnout. But once elected a DA has massive power: Simply by choosing which laws to prosecute aggressively, and which to ignore, a DA can remake law and order in a city overnight.

And sadly, that's exactly what George Soros realized.

Soros is one of the richest men in the world, and the most important left-wing donor in America. Ironically, while he promotes a Radical Left anti-market ideology, Soros made his billion in the financial markets, and he has a keen eye for spotting an undervalued asset. And back in 2016, while most of the country had its eyes on the race between Donald Trump and Hillary Clinton, Soros and his shadowy network of political operatives saw an opportunity. According to a profile in *Politico* published just before the 2016 vote, Soros had discovered the death grip he could have on American politics if he got in at the local level.

"While America's political kingmakers inject their millions into high-profile presidential and congressional contests," the author wrote, "Democratic mega-donor George Soros has directed his wealth into an under-the-radar 2016 campaign to advance one of the progressive movement's core goals—reshaping the American justice system."

The profile goes on to note that every candidate that Soros hand-picked for these races "ran on platforms sharing major goals of Soros', like reducing racial disparities in sentencing and directing some drug offenders to diversion programs instead of to trial."[10]

In otherwise little-watched DA races, Soros found, even a few hundred thousand dollars could have a huge impact, allowing radical leftists to win primaries and then ride the heavily-Democratic tilt of major urban areas to victory. And so, city by city, he began to build his network. In Illinois's massive Cook County, $2 million Soros cash elected Kim Foxx as the very first Soros DA. In Florida's Orange County, home to Orlando, Aramis Ayala was elected with the help of $1.3 million from a Soros PAC.[11] Her conduct quickly became so radical that Florida's Republican governors had to yank her off of several high-profile murder cases, lest she botch them and allow killers to go free.

In the years after 2016, the network grew: San Francisco's George Gascon wore out his welcome there, so he resigned, moved to Los Angeles, and got himself elected DA in *that* city, helped by nearly $3 million from Soros. In Texas, John Creuzot got elected DA of Dallas County with $236,000 from Soros, then promptly decriminalized theft valued at less than $750. Other Soros proteges won office in Harris County (Houston), Bexar County (San Antonio), and Travis County (Austin). According to the Law Enforcement Legal Defense Fund, by late 2022 America had 75 Soros-backed prosecutors, whose domains included half of America's 50 largest cities.[12]

Perhaps the single most famous Soros DA, though, is Larry Krasner, who has been turning Philadelphia into a ruin ever since he got elected in 2017 with a big boost of Soros cash. Before he got into law enforcement, Krasner had a long career *suing* law enforcement in private practice, bringing dozens of cases against cops in Philadelphia when he felt they had violated the law.

There's nothing wrong with doing that, of course, but it does seem a little strange that the man's next move would be to join the very people he'd spent his career suing, no? It's almost as if there was a dark network of left-wing activists pushing him in that direction, attempting to infiltrate the law enforcement infrastructure of Philadelphia and bring it down from the inside.

So far, it's working. In his first week in office, Krasner fired thirty-one of the city's assistant DAs. Krasner took a new, more permissive attitude toward virtually all crimes. In 2015, Philadelphia prosecutors dropped charges in just 17 percent of illegal gun possession cases. By 2021, that figure was at 61 percent.[13] In a city with one of America's worst murder rates, more than half of those caught carrying an illegal gun weren't punished for it.

Under Krasner's stewardship, Philadelphia now has the highest per capita homicide rate among America's ten largest cities—yes, worse than Chicago![14] In 2016, the city's last Krasner-free year, Philadelphia had 277 homicides. In 2021, it had 562, an increase of more than 100 percent.[15] Not only are murders vastly more common, but a larger and larger share are going unsolved. Back in the 1980s, with far less technology available, Philadelphia police "cleared" (that is, solved) about 80 percent of murders. In the years before Krasner, the clearance rate was around 65 percent. Under Krasner, it has dropped below 50 percent.[16] Non-fatal shootings, meanwhile, are solved less than 20 percent of the time.

On the streets of the City of Brotherly Love, carjackings are more common than they've been since the mid-1990s. Retail theft abounds. Citizens walk around scared for their lives, knowing that more criminals are walking around than ever—Krasner's new bail policies mean that thousands more offenders are released each year without paying a cent. The mayhem in Philadelphia has become so dramatic, so undeniable, that in 2022 the Pennsylvania House took the step of formally impeaching Krasner.[17]

Instead of taking responsibility for the mayhem they have unleashed, and perhaps stepping aside so someone competent can do the job, Krasner and his team have taken the usual liberal tactic of blaming racism. In January 2022, the DA's office put out a report claiming that a chief cause of the city's shootings was "systemic racism." Even if you're dumb enough to believe that, the logical takeaway is that under Krasner, racism in Philadelphia has more than doubled since he took over. So hey, Larry, how about letting a nonracist who *opposes* crime do the job?

No one who's been paying attention is surprised by this outcome. According to *Philadelphia* magazine, Krasner has been telling us who he is for decades.

"When he was practicing law in Philadelphia," the 2018 profile says:

> . . . he sued the police department some 75 times. He doesn't believe in the death penalty, and he's called law enforcement "systemically racist." Since taking office, he's ordered his assistant district attorneys to request cash bail less often and include a cost analysis of incarceration when making sentencing recommendations. Krasner talks a lot about "social justice" and "inequality." But you won't hear him mention victims very often. And why? Because Krasner views crime victims as an obstacle to his agenda.[18]

This, in my professional opinion, is spot-on. And it's exactly the opposite of what being a district attorney is about.

When I did the job in Westchester, my office was open 24-7, not for criminals, but for victims and their families. One of my desk drawers was always full of toys, for the tragic occasions when I prosecuted crimes involving children. My coffee pot was always on, and boxes of tissues were always within reach. As the DA, I was a public servant—*their* servant—and I wanted them to feel comfortable sitting with me and telling me their stories. As much as I cared about locking up criminals, my number-one priority, always, was attempting to make the victims of crime whole again. Frequently, a key step in that process was giving the victim my assurance that I would not allow the criminal to victimize them again—that their attacker would be punished for his or her crime, and that he or she would not be allowed to walk free and commit more crimes. At every step in the process, I kept the victims involved and appraised.

Under Krasner and the Soros prosecutors, this duty toward the victims of crime has entirely vanished. For Krasner and the rest, victims only get in the way. Given the agenda they're pushing, I'm not surprised when I hear about victims who have not even been contacted by the prosecutor for their case. This isn't just laziness or sloppiness. It's a betrayal of a prosecutor's moral duty to the victims of crime.

Consider the case of Steven Bernstein. More than forty years ago, Bernstein's brother David was supposed to testify against a serial burglar named Joseph Kindler. Before he could do so, though, David was found dead in the Delaware River, with a concrete block around his neck and two dozen wounds from a baseball bat.[19]

Kindler was convicted and given the death penalty, but was never executed (we've been battling against softheaded liberals on crime for a long time). For the next three decades, Kindler was the exact opposite of a model inmate. He escaped and was recaptured twice. He showed an appalling propensity for violence.

Steven Bernstein and his wife followed every development in Kindler's case. They stayed in touch with the DA's office, checking in every few years, hoping and praying for the day that justice would finally be done for David's death.

Then came Larry Krasner.

In 2018, as one of his first acts in office, one of Krasner's representatives went before a Common Pleas Court and asked the judge to forego the death penalty in Kindler's case in favor of a life sentence. He did so without contacting Steven Bernstein or any other members of the victim's family. Now, Steven is left knowing that his brother's killer will die of old age, living on the taxpayer's dime . . . unless some other, even more liberal court commutes Kindler's sentence again, and lets him die a free man.[20]

Krasner's reign has been particularly infamous, but Soros prosecutors all over the country are producing similar outcomes. In St. Louis, Soros prosecutor Kim Gardner hasn't merely managed to drive up the murder rate. In 2020, her city logged 263 homicides, equal to 87 murders per 100,000 residents.[21] If St. Louis were its own country, it would have *double* the murder rate of the next highest country.

All over the country, the same story is playing out. Justice is doing battle against injustice, and justice is taking a beating. In Chicago, the Soros-appointed prosecutor Kim Foxx has made bail reform and "reimagining prosecution" the focal points of her office's crime policy. All this in a city where, according to The Heritage Foundation, an average of 525 people per year are murdered.[22] Since she was elected as the first Soros prosecutor in 2016, Foxx has dropped all kinds of felony cases. She had directed her office to stop prosecuting shoplifting as a felony as long as the stolen goods were worth less than $1,000. And she is doing it all, in her own words, as part of her pledge "to fight for racial justice."[23] Somehow, when black criminals are let off for crimes against black victims, that is "racial justice." To Kim Foxx, it is the color of a criminal's skin that matters, not the content of their crimes.

A few years after Foxx took office, she famously took it easy on Jussie Smollett, the actor who staged a hate crime against himself, hoping to stoke racial tensions, inflame anti-Trump sentiment, and boost his own acting career. When she heard the story that Smollett was pushing—two rednecks approached him on a freezing single-digit winter night, poured bleach on his head, and placed a noose around his neck while screaming *"This is MAGA Country, [n-word]"*—Foxx thought it all sounded perfectly reasonable. So did future Vice President Kamala Harris, who called the attack "a modern-day lynching" and demanded that justice be served. Of course, in reality *nothing* about the attack made sense. Why would two white guys in MAGA hats go roaming at two in the morning with a container of bleach when it was well below freezing? According to Smollett, the attackers specifically recognized him as an actor from the FX show *Empire*, a drama about the hip-hop business. Why would two violent racists ever watch a show like that, and if they did, why would they carry a noose around just in case they ran into an actor from it to attack?

It was all just as stupid as it sounded. Within hours, police found the men Smollett had hired to attack him. Apparently, Smollett was in negotiations regarding his salary, and was looking for a little publicity to beef up the negotiations.

Obviously, Smollett deserved a harsh punishment for what he did. His actions went far behind simply filing a false police report. In reality, Smollett himself had been the one committing a hate crime. By false accusing two white men of assaulting him and screaming slurs at him, Smollett was intentionally libeling white people as a group, vilifying them in order to enrich himself. Smollett's crime was laughable . . . but it was also heinous.

Not to Kim Foxx, though. Initially, her office tried to drop the case against Smollett entirely, without charges. Foxx said there were evidentiary problems with the case that kept her from prosecuting, which was later revealed to be false. She said Smollett had no criminal background, which was a lie.[24] According to the *New York Post*, Foxx also lied about her extensive contact with Smollett's sister when she learned that Smollett was a suspect in a police investigation.[25] Only after the appointment of a special prosecutor was Smollett finally charged, convicted, and given a sentence of 150 days.

Everything about the Smollett case was a farce from beginning to end. Yet the DA of America's second-largest county believed it, because the fake attack confirmed every fake narrative that the Soros prosecutors, BLM, and the rest of the Radical Left have been pushing for years—that the United States of America is a horrible, racist place where black men are hunted in the streets simply for the color of their skin. It's all a lie, a lie that has fueled the destruction of our once-great cities.

Of all the cities being wrecked by the Soros prosecutors, one of the most heartbreaking is my own city of New York. No city benefited more from the steady drop in America's crime rate during the 90s and 2000s. New York went from being one of the most dangerous large cities in the world to one of the safest. But now, radical prosecutors seem determined to undo all of that. They aren't just allowing crime to rise once again. They are determined to take the victims of crime and transform them into the perpetrators.

In July of 2022, Jose Alba, a sixty-one-year-old man with no criminal history, was working a shift at his Manhattan bodega when he was assaulted by Austin Simon, an ex-con with eight prior arrests for assault, robbery, and domestic violence, then out on parole for assaulting a cop. The conflict started when a woman trying to buy chips with an EBT debit card that didn't work became infuriated. She knocked over items on the counter in the bodega and then ran home to get her boyfriend, Simon, who came back to attack the store owner. Simon stormed into an employee-only area, shoved Alba into a wall, and then stood over him and grabbed him as he tried to get away. Alba defended himself with a knife he desperately grabbed from behind a row of candy bars, stabbing and killing Simon.

In every conceivable way, legally and morally, Alba was in the right to defend himself from being assaulted, maimed, and possibly killed by a far younger, stronger man. But leftie Manhattan DA Alvin Bragg didn't see it that way. His version of justice was to charge Alba with murder and throw him into the bowels of the Rikers Island jail on an impossible bail of $250,000. Only after massive local and national media pressure, a wave of protests by victims' rights groups, and a push by politically connected bodega owners with strong political influence in the Democrat party did Bragg finally relent.[26] Two weeks after the stabbing, the charges against Alba were finally dropped. But Alba himself had had enough. The man who came to New York City to pursue the American dream, mostly successfully, decided he'd had enough and moved back to his home country of the Dominican Republic. According to family, he simply didn't feel safe in America anymore.

While Soros prosecutors wreck the country from coast to coast, they routinely receive cover from a press that shares their core values and assumptions: that victims are irrelevant, and criminals are good—unless, of course, a criminal can be used to land some other political attack.

When Soros prosecutors are called out for their crimes against society, their typical pattern is to stay quiet for a few days, knowing that their allies in the corporate press will sweep everything under the rug soon enough. In the case of Darrell Brooks, this is exactly what happened. News reports published in the aftermath of the attack said only that "a vehicle" had plowed through a crowd during a Christmas parade in Waukesha, neglecting to mention the violent criminal behind the wheel. In a tweet published a few days later, CNN declared, "Waukesha will hold a moment of silence today, marking one week since a car drove through a city Christmas parade, killing six people and injuring scores of others."[27]

Really, CNN? So the red SUV just turned its own keys, floored its own gas pedal, and went on a killing spree like a demonic car in some dime-store horror novel?

Shortly after that tweet went up, the story faded from the headlines, just as the Radical Left knew it would. If Darrell Brooks had been a white supremacist, we might *still* have front-page headlines about his crimes. If he'd used a gun as well, we'd already have legislation named after his victims. But Brooks was *not* a white supremacist. He was the polar opposite, having written insane Facebook posts that white people should be "killed in the streets." And so his crime, and his victims, lie forgotten.

Time Bombs

Need more proof that cop-hating, criminal-loving lawyers can rise to the office of District Attorney and wreck a city? Meet Chesa Boudin, the former DA of San Francisco. Chesa has a rare pedigree for a progressive. His grandfather was a lawyer who once represented none other than Fidel Castro. His parents weren't just lefties . . . they were left-wing *terrorists*, members of the radical anti-government group the Weather Underground. In the late '60s and early '70s, the Weathermen became famous for planting bombs in government buildings. They were against the Vietnam War and explicitly pro-Communist.

When Chesa Boudin was just over one year old, his parents left him with a babysitter so they could go rob a Brinks armored car in suburban New York. When the robbery went wrong, the Weathermen shot and killed two police officers and a security guard. Later, Boudin's parents pled guilty to felony murder, sending them to prison for the rest of his childhood.

While his parents languished behind bars, Chesa was raised by his adoptive parents, Bill Ayers and Bernardine Dohrn, themselves Weather Underground members. For the next eighteen years, little Chesa went to visit his parents in prison, where he was presented with a warped sense of crime and punishment, not to mention anger at the justice system for putting his parents there. One can get a sense of the values he acquired from a piece he wrote for *The Nation* as an adult. In the article, Boudin wrote that "prisons and jails do not promote parenting; they seriously impede it. When a parent commits a crime, the system largely overlooks their parental obligations—and the rights of the children left behind—in favor of punishment."[28]

When he grew up, Boudin attended Yale Law School and then took a job as a public defender. In 2019, he was elected San Francisco's 29th District Attorney. John T. Chisholm, the DA who let Darrell Brooks off on $1,000 bail, cheered Boudin's election, writing that he "couldn't wait to get to work with him."[29]

Right away, Boudin went into the family business, planting bombs at the very foundations of our justice system. He immediately fired experienced gang prosecutors and entirely eliminated *all* cash bail, saying it discriminated against the poor. His leniency toward shoplifters whose antics resulted in looting sprees prompted retail chains to leave the city.

In 2020, Boudin's office dealt with the case of Troy McAlister, a forty-five-year-old man who had been arrested for robbery. At the time of his arrest, McAlister had already been convicted of two felonies—carjacking and another count of robbery—on two separate occasions. Under San Francisco's "Three Strikes" law, McAlister should have served a life sentence for the most recent robbery charge, given that it would have been his third strike. But thanks to a policy that Boudin put in place that February, McAlister wasn't given a life sentence. Instead, Boudin's office negotiated a plea deal, sentenced McAlister to time served, and set him free.

Over the next five months, McAlister was arrested five more times, and released each time as Boudin's office declined to bring charges.

Then, just before midnight on New Year's Eve, McAlister stole a car from a woman he'd met on a dating app, climbed behind the wheel drunk and in possession of a firearm, and ran a red light. He T-boned a car, then slammed into two pedestrians in the crosswalk, killing both.

In the aftermath, Chesa Boudin followed the John T. Chisholm playbook to a T. He admitted that Troy McAlister never should have been on the street in the first place. But like Chisholm, he avoided all responsibility for the attack, saying only that what his office did was "not enough."

Thankfully, one of Chesa Boudin's time bombs finally blew up in his *own* face, just like some of the Weather Underground's used to. On November 9, 2021, voters in San Francisco—in *San Francisco!*—decided they'd had enough. America's most left-wing major city voted to recall its district attorney and chart a new course for their city.

This chapter would not be complete without a quick discussion of George Gascón, Boudin's predecessor as San Francisco DA, who quit the job and moved to Los Angeles in 2019 to become their DA instead. Gascón entered office on a wave of Soros cash with a lot of promises: As DA, he said he would not seek cash bail and would seek to release many currently awaiting bail. He would end charging of juveniles as adults. He announced plans to reevaluate any sentence where the prisoner had already served twenty years, as well as reopen cases of officer-involved shootings that were previously closed.[30]

Just like with Boudin, the results were quick and disastrous. One of Gascón's most famous cases involved an individual by the name of James Tubbs, who was a juvenile when he sexually assaulted two young girls in separate instances. At the time of the crime Tubbs was just two weeks away from turning eighteen. One of his victims, meanwhile, was ten. Tubbs was finally arrested at the age of twenty-six. But then the twist hit: After being arrested, Tubbs began identifying as a woman!

"Hannah" Tubbs pleaded guilty to the crime, but Gascón's office wasn't looking to put a child molester in prison. Instead, holding firm to its promise against charging minors as adults, Gascón's office decided that Hannah would be treated as a minor. The twenty-six-year-old Tubbs was sentenced to two years in a juvenile facility . . . and since "she" was now a "woman," she would be housed with females! The LA Sheriff's office offered to simply hold Tubbs in a county jail instead, but the judge refused to allow it. Tubbs also did not have to register as a sex offender.

Because Gascón failed to send Tubbs to an adult criminal court where s/he rightly belongs, the juvenile facility is left to house a twenty-six-year-old woman for two years. This is criminal privilege.[31]

It's not the only example. William Flores murdered two police officers in a motel shootout in Los Angeles. At the time of the slayings, he was on probation for a charge of carrying an illegal gun. But

Flores could have been in prison for that charge instead . . . except that prosecutors had dropped both drug charges and ammunition enhancements for his illegal gun. Not only that, but the day before the shooting, Flores's parole officer demanded he appear in court for a parole violation involving an assault a week earlier. But Flores wasn't taken into custody, until his life of crime had finally claimed two better men's lives.

Over and over, Gascón's office has refused to prosecute "three strikes" cases where a person is on their third strike, and the conviction would impose mandatory prison time on an offender. Flores's case was just another such example. Gascón said that the sentence Flores received, which allowed him to be free to kill two police officers, was consistent with his office's policy "since the suspected cop killer did not have a documented history of violence."[32] The truth? William Flores was a gang member who previously served two prison stints for burglary and car theft, and had been banned from carrying a gun since 2011. Law enforcement sources reported that this gangbanger was so notorious the police would have recognized him the moment they saw him. George Gascón doesn't think this cop killer should have been in jail because he doesn't have a history of violence? You get a gun, ammunition, methamphetamine, you're already a felon, you steal a vehicle, burglarize a home, commit domestic violence, beat your girlfriend after already doing two prison stints, and this guy has no history of violence? Are you stupid? You let this tattooed-face gangbanger back on the street, and he kills two cops? Then you lie about it?

But that's the amazing thing about criminal privilege. No matter how wretched you are, or how many people you hurt, there will *always* be liberals ready to jump to your defense and insist you get another chance.

The Infringement on the Right to Bear Arms

When in Doubt, Blame Guns

So what lessons have the Radical Left taken from the bloodbath in America's cities? Have they learned that demonizing the police as racist and telling them to stop enforcing the law was a devastating error? Have they realized that cash bail exists for a *reason,* and that by getting rid of it they only free violent maniacs to prey on the public even more? Have they accepted that electing Soros prosecutors to side with criminals over their victims only ensures there will be more criminals and more victims in the future?

Of course not.

As always, they've looked at a problem of their own making and come up with the dumbest explanation possible to exonerate themselves: just blame guns!

For the Radical Left, basically every violent crime can be blamed on either systemic racism or poverty, with the right mental gymnastics. But in the rare cases where that explanation falls short, then the problem *must* be guns. When a crook with three prior felonies sticks up the convenience store while out on bail for his fourth, the Left casts blame on his 9mm pistol—not on the criminal himself, or on the army of enablers who moved heaven and earth to keep him on the streets. Even when they control every part of the process—the judges, the prosecutors, the police—and even when (as usual) a criminal is a Democrat, the Left will never take responsibility. No no, it must be guns, and by extension all gun *owners*, that are the problem. Aren't they the ones who said not to blame all Muslims for the actions of the few?

The Left always lumps responsible gun owners in with those who use guns—typically, illegally-purchased guns—to commit crimes. Actually, that's not true: the Left blames legal gun owners *more* than criminals for gun-related crimes. When Beto O'Rourke stood up during the 2020 primaries and said, "Hell yes, we're going to take your AR-15, your AK-47," he wasn't talking to the drug dealers, gang members, and street thugs.[1] He was talking to the roughly one-third of American adults who bought their guns legally, and follow every law.[2] He was talking to farmers, hunters, and former military officers all over the country. He was talking to the parents who keep weapons to protect their families from violent criminals.

He was talking to you and me.

Because, at heart, that's what they're *really* worried about. If Democrats were simply worried about gun crime, and wanted to cut it as much as possible, they could do that easily. It would simply require *enforcing* the many laws that already exist against carrying and using *illegally owned guns*.

This was the purpose of New York's old policy of "stop and frisk," implemented by (and now disavowed by) Mayor Michael Bloomberg. Stop and frisk was an NYPD policy where police briefly stopped suspicious persons and searched them for illegal guns or drugs. The searches were rarely more intrusive than a pass through the TSA—but they were far more effective at finding criminal contraband. More than 10 percent of stop-and-frisk searches eventually led to a fine or other criminal conviction. Every year, police seized hundreds of illegally-owned guns.

The purpose of the policy wasn't just putting bad guys in jail. It was to make sure that even taking the risk of carrying an illegal gun wasn't worth it.

"The way you get the guns out of the kids' hands is to throw them against the wall and frisk them," Bloomberg said during a speech in 2015. "Because then they say, 'I don't want to get caught,' so they don't bring the gun. They still have a gun, but they leave it at home."[3]

You can see why Bloomberg used to be Republican: he used to be able to use his brain. But then he stopped, which is why he switched to being a Democrat, and why he spent his failed 2020 presidential campaign disavowing one of his most successful policies.

Why won't Bloomberg and the Left use stop and frisk, if they're so worried about illegal guns? Quite simply, because that would mean focusing their efforts on the people who commit crimes. And that's the same reason they won't strictly enforce other laws that could crack down on illegal guns. For example, one of the most common ways that criminals receive guns is simply by getting someone else (a girlfriend, a friend, a parent) to buy the gun on their behalf. This practice is called a "straw purchase," and it's a federal felony. Yet the law goes almost totally unenforced.

But instead of asking Republicans to join them in punishing straw buyers who funnel guns to criminals, Democrats focus on demonizing tens of millions of gun owners, and calling for sweeping national bans and confiscations. Why? Because that's what Democrats *really* want to do about guns: they know that Republicans are more likely to own guns, more likely to use them legally, and more likely to enjoy and appreciate them. They also know that, if they pass a ban, Republicans are more likely to actually obey it than Democrats.

That's the same reason the Left obsesses about banning "assault weapons" (a term they can't actually define). Check any actual data, and the *vast* majority of gun crimes, of any sort, are committed with (illegal) handguns. Rifles like the AR-15 are actually substantially *under*-represented as guns used in crimes. Overall, rifles of *any* kind are used in only 3% of gun murders in the U.S.[4] The overwhelming majority of people who own AR-15s are simply sports enthusiasts, hobbyists, and collectors who pose no threat to anyone. But they're also very disproportionately rural, and white, and conservative, and those are the real reasons the Left wants to seize those guns first.

"First," but certainly not "only." If Beto were to somehow get his way, and Congress passed a ban on "assault weapons," things wouldn't stop there. Remember what happened to all of us in 2020. "Two weeks of social distancing to slow the spread" became months of lockdowns and years of mask and vaccine mandates. Fathers were arrested in front of their children for playing (alone) in public parks. Restaurants that opened their doors to patrons were slapped with fines, and worse.

Give the Left an inch, and they will take ten thousand miles. As it was with Covid, so it will be with guns.

Because, in the end, all of this traces back to power, who the Left thinks should have it (them), who shouldn't (you), and how much they should get to use it (as much as possible).

The core of contemporary Radical Leftism is that ordinary citizens do not know—in fact, are not *capable* of knowing—what's best for themselves or their families. The Left didn't believe that we could make our own choices about when to wear masks, so they forced us to do it everywhere. They don't believe we should have a say in what our children learn in schools, so their lawmakers and unions want to keep parents out of the classroom (and they're threatening to send in the DOJ if they don't listen). They don't believe we can make good choices about what news sources to read and what videos to watch online, so they want to control that information with a DHS disinformation board.

And so it is with guns. The Second Amendment guarantees "the people" their right to keep and bear arms, but to the Radical Left, "the people" is a frighteningly large group of empowered citizens. Some of them might be "deplorables." Others are "bitter" flyover folk who "cling to guns and religion," in the words of Barack Obama.[5] So in the Radical Left's moral universe, the Second Amendment is out.

So who *is* allowed to own guns? Well, there's some debate about that. After a shooting in his city over the Fourth of July weekend, Philadelphia Mayor Jim Kenney said that only the police should have firearms—no one else.

"I was in Canada two weeks ago and never thought about a gun," he said. "The only people I knew who had guns in Canada were police officers. That's the way it should be here."[6]

After saying he would only be happy "when he wasn't mayor anymore," Kenney said he wished he and his liberal buddies could take unilateral action on gun control, but that Congress made such action impossible.

"If I had the ability to take care of guns, I would," he said. "But the legislature won't let us. Congress won't let us."[7]

Well, thank God for that.

Presumably, the action Kenney the Clueless was talking about would have involved outlawing the sale of firearms in Philadelphia, even to law-abiding citizens who want to own guns for their own protection. Why might a law-abiding citizen in Philly want to buy a gun? Well, under Kenney's leadership, Philadelphia murder rate has *doubled*, from 280 the year before he took over to a staggering 562 in 2021.[8] That's both an all-time record for Philadelphia, and enough to make it one of the most dangerous cities in the entire world.

But naturally, law-abiding gun owners—the people Kenney would target with his big sweeping ban—had very little to do with it. A study conducted by the Department of Justice in 2019 found that fewer than 1 in 50 (less than 2 percent) of all state and federal prisoners who'd possessed or used a firearm during their offense had obtained that firearm from a legal, retail source. More than half of those remaining, according to the study, "had either stolen it (6 percent), found it at the scene of the crime (7 percent), or obtained it off the street or from the underground market (43 percent)."[9]

For some reason, liberals do not understand that the people who use guns illegally—the ones they spend almost all of their time coddling and protecting—are probably going to *acquire* them illegally too. And so it is in the City of Brotherly Love. In early 2022, the ATF found that more than 400 illegal guns were brought in through an illegal, underground "Iron Pipeline," a system by which straw buyers purchased guns in bulk in the South and then shipped them up to their criminal associates in northern cities, who then either used the guns themselves, or sold them at a markup on the street to Philadelphia's many, many felons who can't buy at a gun store themselves. Most of these guns, it bears mentioning, were handguns—*not* the assault rifles that Democrats attempt to ban every few minutes.[10]

The sweeping gun bans that the Left wants are not going to make a difference. Not for criminals. They will only matter for the citizens who obey the law . . . and will then find themselves easy prey for the ones who do not.

But as I said a moment ago, that's really the idea. The Left wants to confiscate guns *en masse* not because it will disarm criminals, but because it will disarm conservatives and citizens who may need to defend themselves.

That's why, at the peak of the 2020 George Floyd frenzy, the Left even dabbled with the insane notion of *disarming the police.*

In mid-June, while dozens of American cities were still smoldering from riots, *Time* magazine published an article with the headline "What the U.S. Can Learn from Countries Where Cops Don't Carry Guns." Throughout, the author of this piece (of garbage) suggested that what police officers in the United States really need is to "gain legitimacy and authority by maintaining the respect and approval of the public."[11] The piece promotes a concept called "policing by consent," which says that police should avoid instilling fear in the criminals they fight against. As far as I can tell, this "policing by consent" means that if criminals don't like a bunch of cops being around all the time, then they should leave. Thankfully, the author of this piece was just a *Time* writer instead of Biden's nominee for attorney general . . . but hey, all bets are off for the Kamala administration.

When the Minneapolis City Council moved to abolish the local police department, their plan was to replace it with a "transformative new model for cultivating safety." This "transformative" model revolved around, basically, sending unarmed social workers instead of armed police to as many crime scenes as possible. And then . . . well, it wasn't exactly clear. The thinking seemed to be "Guns and cops bad! Social workers with Oberlin degrees and $200,000 in student loans good!"

But in reality, America will never actually be a *gun-free* country. Not even the Left wants that. What they want is a *gun monopoly*. Starting with the elite Left's bodyguards, of course. At the very same time they were trying to abolish their city's police, Minneapolis city council members Andrea Jenkins, Phillips Cunningham, and Alondra Cano were billing the city $4,500 per *day* for private security.[12] In spring 2022, the *Chicago Sun-Times* revealed that Chicago Mayor Lori Lightfoot didn't just have her personal bodyguard of 20 officers, but an additional "Government Security Detail" from the Chicago PD with 65 officers, five sergeants, and lieutenant. Think Lightfoot is in any hurry to surrender her private army? Of course not—this is the same woman who broke lockdown rules to visit a hairstylist, and said the rules didn't apply to her because "I'm out in the public eye."[13]

So, after the bodyguards, who else gets guns? Given their recent behavior, maybe the FBI would get a pass. Raid the home of a former president, and monitor parents who get a little too loud at school board meetings, and ta da, you get to have a gun too! But if the pendulum ever swings the other way again—if the FBI makes it a priority to, say, investigate real crimes and lock up real criminals again—then I'm sure they will have their guns taken as well.

Even if the Left actually abolished our police, though, we would still have armed enforcers on our streets. They just wouldn't necessarily be *police*. That was one hidden agenda of the push to abolish the police and replace them with new "transformative" models.

The Left understands that the police departments are inherently conservative organizations in America. They promote conservative values, and most officers are themselves at least somewhat conservative. That used to be unremarkable, but today, the Left has near total dominance of tech, media, academia, and the rest of the government bureaucracy. They've even made the military woke. As an even vaguely conservative center of power, police departments are a huge outlier. If they can't be assimilated, then they have to be taken out.

But what if the Left could create new, 100% left-wing "woke" police from scratch? Well then, naturally, there would be no problem giving those people guns.

One of the most honest takes from the Radical Left in 2020 came from Corey Mohler, a radical left-wing software engineer and online cartoonist. Two days after George Floyd's death, Mohler laid out his vision of what should replace the police, and why it would be a superior option.

"If I need to call someone for help or protection it needs to be an institution which I know is [explicitly] and openly on the side of the people against power," Mohler said. "The police cannot be reformed into such an institution, they exist to protect power and property against the people. If a white middle class person calls the police on a poor black person, they need to know the police will side with the black person, by default. This won't happen with a sanitized police force, but only an independent community defense organization, like the Black Panthers."[14]

Armed radicals, with a total monopoly of force, and the power to dispense ad-hoc "justice" based on politics, class, and skin color. It's a radical's dream, one that has been lived out in Mao's China and Bolshevik Russia.

The bottom line is this: the Radical Left does not want ordinary citizens to have any recourse against the government or other potentially violent actors. They want people dependent on the government for protection, just like they want us completely dependent on the government for *everything else*. In their eyes, we are too stupid, or too innately evil, to govern ourselves, to protect ourselves, or to make decisions about our own destinies.

Liberals vs. the Law: Round 342,498,983

If there's one thing you can be certain of, it's that liberals will never pass up an opportunity to exploit a tragedy for political gain—whether it's a terror attack, a global pandemic, or a mass shooting that kills dozens of people. As soon as the event in question takes place, the countdown to the next sober, sad speech from a Democrat who wants "action"— read: some stupid law they could sneak past us otherwise—begins.

In the aftermath of the tragic school shooting in Uvalde, Texas, for instance, Biden spoke to reporters outside the White House lawn before leaving on Marine One. As always, Biden was protected by well-armed Secret Service agents. As he spoke, a man with a sniper rifle kept a silent, watchful vigil at a distance. Biden was safe.

Dressed in his signature aviators, Biden launched into a diatribe against Americans' rights, saying that the Second Amendment to our Constitution "was never absolute" (that's Democrat for "Kiss it goodbye").

"You couldn't buy a cannon when the Second Amendment was passed," he said. "You couldn't go out and purchase a lot of weaponry."[15]

If Joe really wanted to have an honest conversation about the rights of gun owners in the United States, he could have done that. He could have mentioned the fact that he owns several guns himself. He might have mentioned that his son Hunter acquired a handgun illegally by lying and saying he wasn't on drugs. If Joe were serious about stopping the illegal gun purchases that cause so many deaths in America, he could set a great example by starting with his own son.

But Biden did no such thing. Whatever puppeteer was pulling his strings that day wouldn't let him. Instead, he spouted off his talking points, climbed into his helicopter, and waited for the words he had just spoken to travel all over the country, sowing more division and outrage.

But it's not just Biden. By the time Joe Biden began blabbering about cannons from the White House lawn, these stupid arguments had been around for decades. And much like Joe himself, they refuse to just *go away*. So let's see if we can send them out in a hail of bullets once and for all, shall we?

Let's start with Biden's little quip about cannons. As it happens, that little rhetorical flourish is a lie.

According to the historian David Kopel, who was quoted soon afterward in the *Washington Post*, "everything in that statement is wrong. There were no federal laws about the type of gun you could own, and no states limited the kind of gun you could own."[16]

Wait, it turns out that the man who finished near the bottom of his law school class and actually never practiced any real law has a shoddy command of both the Second Amendment's meaning and its history? I'm shocked.

There's another talking point you'll hear at a lot of boring dinner parties, which goes more or less along these lines: "When the Second Amendment was passed, we only had *muskets*. Therefore, only muskets and the like are protected by the Amendment. The thousands of more powerful and more advanced guns that exist today are not covered."

The people making this argument sometimes follow up by suggesting, only half seriously, that American citizens today are well within their rights to carry colonial muskets, while all other firearms should be banned by the government. But hey, if you want to carry a black-powder musket around to protect yourself on the streets of Chicago, be our guest!

You might think I'm exaggerating, but this argument really is made all the time. In July 2022, two liberal law professors made this case in a joint op-ed for the *New York Times*.

"Modern guns are vastly more powerful than colonial-era muskets, yet [Supreme Court] Justice [Clarence] Thomas indicated that these contemporary weapons presumptively fall within a category of constitutionally protected 'arms,'" the two wrote. At another point, they ask "Is a modern AR-15-style rifle relevantly similar to a colonial musket? In what ways?"[17]

I'm so glad they asked. First, the musket of the 1790s was the primary weapon of war carried by colonial militias. Today, the primary weapon of war carried by our military is the "AR-15-style rifle." Like it or not, the Second Amendment, properly understood, *does* protect the right of private citizens to carry weapons that our military carries.

It really is that simple.

But if you insist on digging down into the gritty legal details, I'm more than happy to grab my shovel and do so.

When you read our Constitution, (or any legal statute, for that matter), it's important that you pay attention to each word and phrase. Often, these words are the result of days or months of careful debate among very smart people. The language of our laws was chosen for a reason, and everything about that language—from the specific words used to the order in which they are used—matters. So does the etymology, usage history, and intent behind each of those words.

Consider the full text of our Second Amendment:

A well regulated Militia being necessary to the security of a free State, the right of the people to keep and bear Arms, shall not be infringed.[18]

By now, most people have heard these words so many times that they don't think about what they mean. But as with all our rights, the wording is tremendously important. You might notice, for instance, that the amendment does not say the people "*shall have* the right to keep and bear arms." In other words, it doesn't confer a right that previously did not exist. On the contrary, the Second Amendment (much like the First) says that the right of the people to keep and bear arms could not be *infringed upon* by the government. The right itself, in the Framers' eyes, already existed, with its roots deep in the English Common Law.

There were good reasons for this. Perhaps more than any group in history, the Founders knew how important it was for citizens to be able to protect themselves and their families—from criminals, from invading armies, and yes, from the government. The late Justice Antonin Scalia, who famously did many hours of historical research before even beginning to write an opinion, has noted that the Framers would have been keenly aware that "the Stuart kings [of England] had destroyed the people's militia, not by disbanding it, but by disarming those of its members whom they disfavored."[19]

In other words, the right of the people to have weapons was well understood to be fundamental and innate at the time of the

Founding. Without it, the people had absolutely no recourse against the government, or against rogue bands of criminals who might wish to do them harm.

You might also notice that as a whole, the structure of our Second Amendment is technically ungrammatical, at least by the standards of modern English. The initial dependent clause—known in legal circles as the "militia clause"—does not logically lead into the clause that follows it, sometimes known as the "bear arms" clause. If you were forced to diagram sentences as a student, as I was, you might get the urge to rewrite the whole thing so that it would more accurately reflect the way we speak and write today.

But the Framers of our Constitution were not writing in modern English. They were continuing a tradition that extended back to the founding of England, a time when such prefatory clauses were common. As the Supreme Court ruled in *District of Columbia v. Heller*, a case that concerned the right of citizens in Washington, D.C., to carry handguns, the first part of this sentence does not "limit the latter [part] grammatically, but rather announces a purpose."[20]

That purpose, as the Supreme Court ruled in that case, was to ensure that private citizens would have the same right to bear weapons "in common use" in the present day as citizens in the eighteenth century had to bear weapons that were "in common use" in *their* day. There were exceptions to this right, of course, as there are exceptions to most rights. There are laws, for instance, which prohibit the possession of firearms by the mentally ill, just as there are laws which prohibit people from possessing "dangerous and unusual weapons."

But these limitations do not change the fundamental meaning of the Second Amendment. As the Supreme Court has ruled:

... the conception of the militia at the time of the Second Amendment's ratification was the body of all citizens capable of military service, who would bring the sorts of lawful weapons that they possessed at home to militia duty. It may well be true today that a militia, to be as effective as militias in the 18th century, would require sophisticated arms that are highly unusual in society at large. Indeed, it may be true that no amount of small arms could be useful against modern-day bombers and tanks. But the fact that modern developments have limited the degree of fit between the prefatory clause and the protected right cannot change our interpretation of the right.[21]

So the next time Aviator-Shades Biden or someone annoying at a house party tells you that your right to own a gun only applies to a gun that Daniel Boone might have used, I suggest directing them to the Supreme Court opinion above.

Then again, if Biden's poor performance in law school is any indication of his reading comprehension skills, I don't know that it would help much.

And by the way: Even if we granted the strange premises of this silly muskets argument, liberals would *still* be wrong. Because, in fact, muskets were *not* the only firearms available at the time our Constitution was written. As one historian of colonial weaponry has pointed out, "firearms that can hold larger capacities of ammunition and operate at faster rates of fire . . . have existed in the United States and its preceding colonies well before the drafters of the Constitution even bore the thought to bring quill to parchment." In fact, "some early firearms boasted mechanics designed to provide multiple shots without reloading, primarily through the addition of multiple barrels or locks. . . . While primitive, the first of these repeating arms were seen in development as early as the 14th century, some 400 years before the creation of the Bill of Rights."[22]

Most importantly, these guns were made so that private citizens would have an easier time shooting—whether for sport, hunting, or self-defense. There is a reason that our Founding Fathers did not refer to "muskets" when they wrote our Second Amendment. Despite what the modern Radical Left might say, these men were smart. They didn't make mistakes, and they didn't overlook any details when it came to the framing of our Constitution. If they had intended to protect only the right to bear muskets—or to bear knives, or sticks, or bows and arrows—then they would have written that.

Repeatedly, no matter how many times they are presented with evidence to the contrary, Biden and the Democrats continue to misunderstand the United States Constitution. When it suits their political purposes, they claim the Constitution is a "living document" that is supposed to change as society changes. Yet when it comes to guns, the liberals become hyper-literal: The Second Amendment *must* mean only what it meant on the exact day it was adopted by colonists in the eighteenth century.

In March of 2018, the argument came from no less a figure than retired Supreme Court Justice John Paul Stevens, who said that the "civic engagement" he had seen from schoolchildren after the mass shooting at Parkland High School "demanded our respect." In response to this tragedy, he implored gun activists to seek a full repeal of the Second Amendment, calling any concerns about the right of people to defend themselves against the government "a relic of the 18th century."[23]

This hyper-literalism comes into play with another routine liberal claim about the Second Amendment: that the amendment doesn't protect a private right of gun ownership, but only the right of the people, collectively, to form militias for national defense. This argument does not make any sense, and it never has. But whenever there is a mass shooting, you'll be sure to see it pop up again.

Make no mistake: these people will not stop until the only people in this country who have guns are their private security guards, the FBI, ideologically-controlled enforcers, and criminals. They know that citizens without guns are powerless. In this way, they are no different than the old Stuart kings of England, who believed that people who possessed the wrong political opinions were too dangerous—and, in some cases, too stupid—to be trusted with weapons for the purposes of their own defense.

Luckily, more Americans than ever have begun to see through the partisan, power-grabbing tactics of the Radical Left. As terror groups such as Black Lives Matter and Antifa wrought havoc on the streets of our major cities throughout 2020, more Americans than ever rushed to their local gun shops to arm themselves. That year, more than 22 million guns were sold in the United States, topping the previous record of 16 million that was set in 2016 (the *last* year that the Radical Left engaged in widespread rioting and looting). But it wasn't just the pandemic. Although firearm sales have declined slightly since the pandemic, a recent study has found that "as of June 2022, firearm sales in the United States have passed the one million mark each month for nearly three straight years. . . . According to the FBI's National Instant Criminal Background Check System (NICS), there have been 35 straight months of sales in excess of one million units."[24]

The Radical Left used Soros prosecutors and the lies of BLM to unleash the worst crime surge in American history. In response, the American people have asserted one of their central rights, and taken their protection into their own hands. And Beto O'Rourke can only pout and fume.

This is important for every American. But it's especially important for women.

The Silver Bullet

Consider what happened on the Upper East Side of Manhattan on the evening of June 29, 2022. Mayor Eric Adams met with *New York Times* columnist Maureen Dowd so he could walk her through his "nightlife routine." That night, said routine included a twenty-year-old woman being shot in the head, execution-style, while pushing her baby in a stroller on the Upper East Side of Manhattan. Almost immediately, Mayor Adams rushed to the scene, making sure to bring Dowd along with him. As soon as he arrived, he launched into a speech blaming guns for this tragedy.

"More guns in our city means more lives lost," he said. "It means more babies crying as those who love them lie dead."[25]

In the days to come, the details would come to light. The victim, whose name was Azsia Johnson, had been lured to the park by her abusive ex-boyfriend, who was also the father of her child. He had tricked her into coming to the park by saying that he had items for the baby. Then he walked up behind her and shot her in the head. A few weeks before this crime had occurred, Azsia had filed a domestic violence complaint against the man who would soon kill her. She was given no help from the NYPD, according to her family.

That Mayor Adams—a man who seemed reasonable when he was campaigning for the job—would come out and trash guns instead of the shooter shows just how clueless this former police captain is about domestic violence.

But Adams may at least have more of a clue than his state's governor, Kathy Hochul, who fell into the job when her predecessor Creepy Andrew Cuomo got drummed out for sexual harassment. Hochul has vowed to fix New York's self-inflicted increase in crime with a raft of new gun legislation to address the problem. After making this outrageous assertion, the Accidental Governor was asked whether she had numbers to back up her claims.

"I don't need numbers," she said. "I don't need to have a data point to say this. I know that I have a responsibility for this state to have sensible gun safety laws."[26]

Hochul said that just a week after the Supreme Court threw out her state's stringent gun laws in its landmark *New York State Rifle and Pistol Association v. Bruen* decision. Hey, Kathy! Have a little humility!

But to these people, the law doesn't matter. The Supreme Court doesn't matter, and neither does anything they say. By virtue of not being liberal enough, the Court has become "illegitimate." During Biden's first two years, most of the Left wanted him to pack the Supreme Court with new justices, who would then rubberstamp insane views about firearms, abortion, and the Constitution in general. If that had happened, liberals like Mayor Adams and Governor Hochul would get the world they have always dreamed of—one where no law-abiding citizen can carry a gun, where the only people who *do* have guns are the criminals who are willing to gun people down in the street.

If this ever happens, thousands of people will suffer. And women will be hit particularly hard.

During my career in law enforcement, I have seen unbelievable amounts of violence. Much of it was done against women. On the surface, the reasons are obvious. Women are typically smaller and physically weaker than men, and throughout history, that has made us victims. When I was the District Attorney in Westchester County, I frequently met with women who'd been beaten by their husbands, their boyfriends, and sometimes complete strangers. As a judge, I tried the cases of men who'd murdered their wives and girlfriends with their bare hands. Some cases involved men who had simply seen a woman on the street, followed her for a few blocks, and then decided—unprompted—to rape and kill her.

Like it or not, these things are possible in the world we live in. Down on the streets of our major cities—the ones that aren't visible from the skyscraper suites where liberal media networks decide what stories to cover—such attacks occur with alarming frequency. They always have, and now they're happening more than they have in decades.

Women make up a disproportionate number of abuse victims in this country—and every country, for that matter. Every year, millions of women are abused by men who have an immense physical advantage over them. They are shot, stabbed, beaten, and sexually assaulted. In many cases, the only protection women have against these assaults is a firearm.

It's no wonder that over the past few years, women have bought more firearms than they have at any other point in history. Between January of 2019 and April of 2021, according to one study, more than 3.5 million women became first-time gun owners.[27] During the same period, about 50 percent of new gun purchases were made by women, and about 90 percent of people who own gun shops reported an increase in women who bought guns. In fact, according to the same study, one of the fastest growing groups of gun owners in this country was black women, many of whom live in the very communities that were hit hardest by the rioting and looting during the Summer of Floyd. And if the police didn't or couldn't respond, women gun owners were ready to defend themselves and their families.

When you look back at the footage from that summer, watching mobs breaking windows and kicking down the doors of small businesses, it becomes crystal clear why these women felt a need to arm themselves. They saw, viscerally and indisputably, that police would not always be there to protect them. When things got bad enough, or the politics became toxic enough, the police would retreat or be overwhelmed, and then every citizen would have to look out for himself . . . or herself.

Without firearms, the strongest man wins every fight. It's that simple.

With firearms, the story changes. With a firearm on her person, the woman has at least a fighting chance of taking down the man who wants to beat or kill her. It is not an exaggeration to say that when it comes to physical altercations, guns can be the difference between life and death for women.

They can be a silver bullet.

I've seen it happen. And it will happen more in the future . . . unless the Left has its way, and forces all of us to be helpless victims instead.

Illegal Crossings

During his 2020 campaign, Joe Biden said that if he were elected president, one of his top priorities would be to "safely reopen America."[1] That fall, he posted "an eight-part plan to make sure the reopening is safe and strong and sets the foundation for an economy that works for everyone."[2] We all thought he was working to open schools and businesses, essentially giving us back our pre-pandemic freedom.

But instead, he has reopened America in a bizarre way that was shocking to all but the Radical Left. He kept trying to keep us masked on all public transportation. He insisted that businesses with more than 100 employees and the U.S. military require vaccinations of everyone. He didn't reopen America the way the public *wanted*.

Americans tired of the pandemic welcomed the reopening of America. Little did they know that the opening had nothing to do with them and everything to do with illegal entry by anyone simply wanting to come here.

When Biden took office in January of 2021, the number of illegal immigrants encountered by Border Patrol was hovering between 70,000 and 80,000 per month. This number was already much higher than normal, and our Border Patrol were having trouble coping with the high volume of migrants. But Biden wasn't concerned. This, after all, is a man who ran on a promise to "rescind the un-American travel and refugee bans" put in place by the previous administration, and to "immediately reverse the Trump administration's cruel and senseless policies" of having a border exist.[3] Biden said his administration would "welcome immigrants in our communities" and "reassert America's commitment to asylum-seekers and refugees."[4]

Biden's rhetoric might have talked about restoring America's values. But his actual policies as president have a very different practical outcome: the destruction of America itself. During his first weeks in office, President Biden signed a wave of executive orders that effectively opened our southern border to the entire world. One order immediately halted the ongoing construction of President Trump's border wall. In one of my visits to the border, I personally viewed construction material on pallets along with metal braces sitting and rotting along with President Trump's plans to close off the border. There was no security, there was no fence around the material, and Border Patrol told me there were millions of dollars in construction material laid open for anyone who wanted them.

Another order ended Trump's "zero tolerance" policy requiring criminal prosecution of those illegally crossing the border. Yet another revoked Trump's 2017 order barring visas for those from several countries linked to radical Islamic terrorism, such as Libya, Somalia, and Yemen. While President Trump had issued a stronger "public charge rule" preventing immigrants on welfare from receiving permanent U.S. residency, Biden ordered the rule to be gutted once again.

Some orders that Biden signed were even more far-reaching. One order required that the "root causes" of mass migration be addressed—such an important task that it was handed off to the Cackler-in-Chief, Vice President Kamala Harris, who's made so many fumbles I'm amazed that the woman even shows up in public. Now we assume that everyone crossing is a public charge and will rely on the cornucopia of benefits that America blesses her own citizens with. Another called on federal agencies to "eliminates sources of fear and other barriers that prevent immigrants from accessing government services available to them."[5]

At the signing ceremony for some of his orders, Biden said he was undoing "the moral and national shame of the previous administration," by which he meant policies designed to follow federal law, deter mass migration, and keep refugees safe at the border.[6] I'm sure if he could have signed an order that created a high-speed rail line from Guatemala to El Paso, he'd have done that too.

Of course, the orders he *did* sign did plenty of damage on their own.

In March of 2021, DHS Secretary and future self-appointed "Minister of Truth," Alejandro Mayorkas, claimed with a straight face that the border was "closed." The month before he said that, in February 2021, Border Patrol encountered more than 100,000 illegal immigrants at our southern border, an increase of 20,000 from the previous month. That March, the number shot up to 173,277, then to 178,795 in April.[7]

In April of 2022, Mayorkas went back on television to beg people to stop coming over his "closed" border. He went before Congress and called any suggestion that the border was open was "offensive." That month, the number of illegal encounters at the border hit 234,088, the highest number of monthly border encounters in twenty-two years. In the 2022 fiscal year, the Border Patrol encountered more than 2.4 million people, not counting the approximate 900,000 got-aways, the highest figure ever in the history of this country. Biden owns that.

Those numbers shot up so fast, you would think there were signs and billboards at the border reading, "C'mon, everybody [you insert any language]! Free food, housing, education and medication. Love, Joe Biden."

How did the numbers explode so quickly? In America, the mainstream press gaslights the American people and tries to convince us that Biden is doing his best to fix the border. Better yet, they might do one better and simply not mention the border at all. But in the rest of the world, there is no such narrative control. From the most impoverished village in Haiti to the most dilapidated slum in Venezuela, the word has gotten out: Joe Biden's America has an open door, and if you show up to it and say the right words, nothing will stop you from getting in.

Ironically, during this same period, Biden fought to implement brand new Covid-19 restrictions on American citizens. In November 2021, his administration attempted to force any business with more than one hundred employees to make vaccination mandatory as an emergency temporary standard under OSHA laws. When a federal judge in Florida declared airport mask mandates unconstitutional, his administration vowed to appeal the decision in court, citing concerns about "U.S. Covid-19 community levels" and the danger of "novel variants."[8]

You're kidding right? We have to wear masks, but immigrants don't? They weren't even *tested* for Covid, and if they were offered vaccines, they could refuse them.

Biden is allowing millions of people, many already sick, who haven't been tested for Covid to walk straight into our country without masks or vaccines. And no, they're not confined or required to stay in one place. They can literally go anywhere they want. Why is Joe Biden willing to allow illegals who are unvaccinated, not tested for Covid, and not required to wear a mask come into this country and spread Covid if they have it? The answer is that he is intentionally allowing Americans who come in contact with these untested, unvaccinated illegals who may have Covid to contract a virus that is so dangerous that requires you lose your job if you're not vaccinated.

It's no wonder that during Joe Biden's first months in office, some migrants crossed the border wearing Biden-themed T-shirts.

In July of 2021, Axios reported that "about 50,000 migrants who crossed the southern border illegally have even been released in the United States without a court date." The report notes that although these people are told to report to local ICE offices instead of court, "just 13 percent [had] shown up so far."[9]

Surprise, surprise.

Since then, hundreds of thousands more illegal immigrants have been set free under similar circumstances. Many of them are placed in ATD, or "Alternative to Detention" programs. In theory, ATD is supposed to use technology to look after migrants after they are released into the country. Many of these illegals are given smartphones, which supposedly track their movements—unless, of course, they decide to toss those smartphones in a river somewhere (or simply turn them off) and keep on walking.

It doesn't have to be this way. Under a policy known as Title 42, implemented by Trump at the start of the Covid pandemic, Border Patrol had the authority to deport most illegals with no questions asked. But Biden, whose only objective was to undo all the progress made during the Trump years, had other plans. On April 1, 2022, the Biden administration announced that it would be ending Title 42. In a press release, a representative of the administration said, "After considering current public health conditions and an increased availability of tools to fight Covid-19 (such as highly effective vaccines and therapeutics), the CDC Director has determined that an Order suspending the right to introduce migrants into the United States is no longer necessary."[10]

This announcement came even as the Biden administration was still fighting to enforce a mask mandate for federal buildings. It came at the same time that border crossings were hitting their highest level ever. And as soon as the announcement was made, the Department of Homeland Security began preparing for 18,000 *new* border crossings per day, up from the already 7,000 per day they were seeing at the time.[11]

Thankfully, shortly before the "Grand Opening" date of May 23, a federal judge in Louisiana ruled that the Biden administration's attempt to ram through a repeal of Title 42 violated administrative law. But this decision was only the opening salvo in what quickly became a long legal battle, with Biden and the liberals fighting tooth and nail to lift this policy which would allow torrents of illegals to continue to come through. Just before the close of 2022, the Supreme Court put a longer stay on the administration's effort.

In response to this ruling, and others holding up Biden from ending Trump's highly-successful "Remain in Mexico" policy for asylum seekers, several liberal commentators have tried to argue that our immigration system is "broken." The perpetual chaos and human flood along the Rio Grande, they say, is the fault of the previous administration, and bad laws, and a failure to address the "root causes."

Well, they're almost right on that one. Our immigration system is broken and in need of reform, but not for the reasons liberals say. It's not that America has no immigration laws. We have plenty, and always have. What we lack is a will to enforce them. Even this refusal to enforce the law is codified in government policy.

As soon as Biden took office, he announced a 100-day freeze on deportations from the United States. Why? Liberals want an open border with the world. The message is out, it's being well received and as a result we are suffering an onslaught of illegals, about whom we know nothing, in the southern part of our country.

Biden doubles down on the chaos by not enforcing existing laws, attempting to repeal them in court, and then breaking them as a last resort. His administration releases hundreds of thousands of people into the United States without court dates who then play telephone with their friends at home to come to America.

And it's all happening in broad daylight.

If you really want to be shocked, consider what they're doing in the dead of night, when they think no one is looking.

Night Flights

In January 2022, my cohosts and I on *The Five* viewed a newly released video going viral online. It had clearly been recorded secretly, for reasons that would soon become obvious.

The video showed a group of men standing on the runway of Westchester County Airport in New York, not far from where I live. It was in the early morning hours that a private flight from Texas had just landed. As the passengers—who, we would soon learn, were all illegal immigrants—were being transferred from that plane to a bus, the men talked.

"You don't want to be somewhere where the spotlight is there," one of them said. "You want to be as down-low as possible. A lot of this is just down-low stuff that we don't tell people because what we don't want to do is attract attention. We don't want the media. Like, we don't even know where we're going when they tell us."

Asked why they had to conduct this operation in the dead of night, one of the men said, "You know why. Look who's in office. That's why."

"What's the big secret?" asked the man filming.

"Because if this gets out, the government is betraying the American people."[12]

Drawing on my law enforcement and airport contacts, I had reported about flights leaving in the middle of the night and landing hours later in Westchester County. I had learned that these planes were all full of illegal immigrants, mostly young men and some children. After these people left the planes, they were ferried to facilities on Long Island, Connecticut, and New Jersey. There were many such flights. One transported the illegals to a Portchester Costco in Westchester County, New York.

In October of 2021, a photograph of one of these planes landing in Westchester was featured on the cover of the *New York Post* under the headline "Biden's Secret Flights." The story reported that "around 2,000 of the underage migrants have arrived at the airport outside White Plains on 21 flights since August 8."[13]

That turned out to just be the tip of the iceberg.

Given that these flights are conducted in secret, it's extremely difficult to get an accurate count of just how many people have been ferried into the interior of the United States in this shady, clandestine manner. If the Biden administration doesn't think it's doing anything wrong by ferrying these people into cities and towns all over the country, then why would they do it in the middle of the night?

Why? First, it's yet another way to hide the scale of what is happening to this country. America is a big country with a lot of people. But even for a country of this size, millions of people pouring in over just a couple of years will attract attention. The border itself is far away for most of us, and as long as the press deliberately keeps its cameras away, most people won't notice it. But if dozens of flights bringing migrants into your city, and every city, were done in broad daylight? Americans would realize what is happening to their country.

Second, they do this in secret because they *know* that these people haven't been properly vetted. They know there's a good chance that some are undesirable, if not worse. Millions of us want to know who's coming into our country, and if they pose a threat.

I've talked with parents who are still mourning children who've been murdered by criminal illegals, and I've reported the stories of the victims. On a smaller scale, I've visited the border three times, and I've listened to people who live in the southern border towns of the United States—the ones who are often the first to suffer when waves upon waves of illegal immigrants show up at our borders and begin moving in.

Most people who live in places like New York City, D.C., or the Bay Area never have to think about these things. They assume that anyone who complains about the thousands of immigrants pouring over our southern border *must* be racist.

What's Good for the Goose . . .

Beginning in the summer of 2022, a few southern governors decided to change that. First, Governor Greg Abbott of Texas began sending busloads of migrants up to wealthy liberal enclaves in New York and the nation's capital. Three of the buses went to the Naval

Observatory, home of Kamala Harris, the supposed "Border Czar" who had been charged by Biden with keeping things secure.[14]

But the hypocrisy really began when Governor Ron DeSantis took fifty Florida-bound migrants and instead rerouted them to Martha's Vineyard, the small island off the coast of Massachusetts that has been a favorite vacation spot for rich, pro-immigration liberals for decades.

Almost within minutes of the migrants' arrival, local liberals began to see reality, and complain loudly about it. One of them said that Martha's Vineyard was "not the best place for [these people] to start fresh." Another said that there was "no place to live here," and that "housing is bad."

"We don't have the services to take care of 50 immigrants, and we certainly don't have housing—we are in a housing crisis," said Lisa Belcastro, operator of the Vineyard's winter shelter. Despite Belcastro's claims, it's likely that nowhere in America is better-suited to absorb the influx of a few dozen migrants, as the Vineyard's permanent population of just 17,000 manages to host hundreds of thousands of visitors in the summer. Not only that, but the state certainly had the money. As a writer at Fox News pointed out, there was enough money in the Massachusetts budget to "give all 50 migrants their own room for an entire year at the Vineyard's swanky $500-per-night Harbor View Hotel."[15]

But this was never a matter of mere money. It's a matter of liberals being completely disconnected from reality. They believe that they can support policies that wreak havoc on communities in the South and Southwest of this country—where people actually have to deal with the thousands of new, unvetted immigrants who show up every day—and never have to feel the effects of those policies.

Recently governors in Texas and Arizona have been urged to make declarations and use their war powers to order police or the National Guard to remove illegal immigrants to Mexico. In Arizona, Article I of the state constitution allows states to engage "in war" when actually invaded. An invasion would permit the state to engage in defensive actions within its own territory or near the border. They allege that violence and lawlessness at the border caused by transnational cartels and gangs satisfies the definition of an invasion. They are correct. A United Nations migration study deems "2021 was the deadliest year at the U.S.-Mexico border."[16]

And our president is working to keep those borders open.

A Day in the Life: Border Patrol

Let's take a look at a single day at the southern border while Joe is president—specifically, April 20, 2022. Winter had ended, and the border was in the absolute peak migrant period of late spring to early summer.

That morning, Border Patrol agents on a routine patrol in the border town of Falfurrias, Texas, encountered a Salvadoran national attempting to enter the country illegally. A background check revealed that the man was a member of the 18th Street Gang, a group known as "one of the most violent street gangs and one of the most prolific in the United States," according to a former official from the Bureau of Alcohol, Tobacco, Firearms and Explosives.[17] Luckily, this particular member was caught, imprisoned, and prepared for deportation.

A few hours later, agents with the Rio Grande City Station came across a group of five migrants from Honduras. Record checks, according to reporting in Shore News Network, revealed that one of the five was convicted of "criminal sexual conduct and sentenced to 36 months' probation . . . and also served two years' incarceration for being unlawfully present in the U.S. after a deportation."[18]

Just a few hours after *that*, Border Patrol agents in McAllen, Texas apprehended a Salvadoran man who'd been convicted of rape in 2018 and given a three-year prison sentence. Apparently, he had served out that sentence, packed his things, and headed right to the United States.

You might argue that these people were caught, and that they are perfect examples of the system working as it should. They attempted to enter the country illegally, and they were apprehended by Border Patrol agents, who performed the necessary background checks and stopped them.

But consider these are just the ones we caught (and my friends in the Border Patrol are unequivocal that huge numbers of crossers are not caught). And this was on *one day*, chosen almost at random. On another day less than a month later, Rio Grande Valley Sector agents arrested three criminal migrants and six gang members. The next day, they arrested a Colombian national convicted of "murder for hire charges" in New York.[19] In the first twenty months of Joe Biden's time in office alone, the brave men and women of our Border Patrol apprehended a stunning 98 people who were already on the terrorist watchlist, and thousands more who had been convicted of crimes in their home countries.[20]

Several of them, such as the one who was arrested in Rio Grande on April 20, had managed to get into the United States undetected before, only being forced to leave when they were caught during routine patrols by law enforcement. And these are the people we *know* about. Recent estimates indicate that around 2,000 people per day, known as "gotaways," manage to cross the border without Border Patrol ever even encountering them.

All of this is happening while Title 42, a law designed to drastically reduce the number of migrants who can enter this country, was supposedly in full effect.

In April of 2022, with rumors swirling that Biden was about to end Title 42, Fox News's Peter Doocy asked Jen Psaki whether her boss was concerned that any of these 2,000 people per day—totaling around 600,000 since Biden was first sworn in—might also be involved in terrorist activities.

She brushed his concerns aside.

"Here's what we're talking about," she said. "Encounters we know of and suspected terrorists attempting to cross, they're very uncommon."

When Doocy followed up by asking whether the president was worried about "holes in the southern border being exploited by people trying to come in and kill Americans," Psaki let slip one of her best all-time great lies from her tenure as press secretary.

"He's grateful," she said, "to the Border Patrol for doing their job and stopping these people and preventing them from getting into the country."[21]

You tell me if Joe Biden is grateful to our Border Patrol.

The Ministry of Truth, Southern Division

In September of 2021, Border Patrol agents on horseback rode up to the banks of the Rio Grande River in Del Rio, Texas, where a large group of Haitian migrants were attempting to rush the border. The town of Del Rio, which is connected to Mexico by bridge, is an unusual entry point. Migrants don't generally show up there. But after the president of Haiti was assassinated in September of 2021, the city was beset by hordes of immigrants who believed that with Biden in the White House, they would be allowed to walk right in.

Thankfully, Border Patrol agents rode to the scene, attempting to round up as many migrants as possible, not to stop them, but to process and vet them. At one point, attempting to catch a person who was attempting to run around his horse to evade capture, one agent took the reins of his horse and swung them in the air. He didn't strike anyone with them, nor did he gesture that he wanted to. Eventually, the agents managed to apprehend most of the people who were attempting to gain entry into the United States that day.

Few people noticed that a photographer was standing just a few yards away on the Mexican side of the river, snapping pictures of the chaos as it unfolded. The photographer, Paul Ratje, eventually sold those photos to the global news network AFP. Within hours, they were everywhere. In one of them, a Border Patrol agent can be seen holding his reins aloft on horseback as a man runs in the opposite direction. If that was the only photo you saw of the incident—and for most people, it was—you might have believed that the reins were a whip, and that the agent was about to strike the fleeing migrant with them.

But even a few seconds of research would reveal no one had "whipped" anyone that day. All a person had to do was click the small arrow on the right-hand side of their laptop screen labeled "next photo," and the whole thing would have been cleared right up. But even if that photo didn't exist, the entire matter only required a moment of thought. Come on, a *whip?* In 2022? When have you ever seen law enforcement carrying a whip around?

At the very least, the president of the United States—a man who is supposedly "grateful" for the work that the Border Patrol does every day—could have issued a statement letting the people of this country know the truth. His administration could have defended its rank-and-file law enforcers. Or, at a bare minimum, it could have paused before making wild claims about the incident to further their own pro-chaos, anti-borders agenda.

But that's not what happened. Instead, Joe Biden attacked his own border agents.

"I promise you," he said, "these people will pay. There will be an investigation underway now, and there will be consequences. There will be consequences. It's an embarrassment, but beyond embarrassment, it is dangerous. It's wrong, it sends the wrong message around the world. It sends the wrong message at home. It's simply not who we are. . . . I take responsibility. I'm president, but it was horrible what you saw, to see people treated like they did, horses barely running them over, people being strapped. It's outrageous."[22]

So, Joe, there's an investigation "underway now," but you've already decided that what happened was "wrong," "horrible," "outrageous" and "there will be consequences"? To me, it sounds like you know that these men did nothing wrong, and you're trying to convict them in the press before the results of any real investigation can come out.

Within hours, Biden's Clown Team was in on the action. Vice President Kamala Harris said she was "deeply troubled" about what went on in Del Rio.

"What I saw depicted about those individuals on horseback treating human beings the way they were was horrible," she said (always a way with words, that Kamala).[23]

Next came Rep. Ilhan Omar, then Alexandria Ocasio-Cortez. Rep. Maxine Waters said that Border Patrol was "trying to bring us back to slavery days and worse than that."[24] You read that correctly:

worse than slavery. The most ridiculous commentary of all, though, came from DHS Secretary Alejandro Mayorkas, the man supposedly in charge of the Border Patrol. He, too, said the images were "horrifying" and that they "painfully conjured up the worst elements of our nation's ongoing battle against systemic racism."

I'm sorry, but what does any of this have to do with racism? The people in those photos were attempting to break the law, and the officers on horseback were doing their jobs by attempting to stop them. Nothing about the story had anything to do with race . . . except to the extent that the Left equates any belief in borders with belief in the Klan.

Keep in mind, by the way, that just a few months after libeling his own agents as racist whip-crackers, Secretary Mayorkas would be the one pushing for a "Disinformation Governance Board." In a press release accompanying the board's creation, Mayorkas said such a board was necessary to "address this threat" posed by online misinformation . . . in particular, misinformation about the border![25] How curious that Mayorkas didn't seem to give a damn about "the threat of misinformation" when it was his own office telling the lies?

When Biden first pronounced his own border agents to be guilty without trial, Mayorkas said that the subsequent "investigation" would be conducted in "days, not weeks." But in the end, that was another untruth. It would be a full nine months before the investigation came out. When it did, the final report was some five hundred pages long. Not a single page contained even a shred of evidence to support what Biden, Harris, and the rest of the left-wing mafia said about those agents. Video evidence conclusively showed that none of the agents had whipped anyone, nor had they threatened to do any such thing. Paul Ratje, the photographer who'd taken the original images that eventually went viral, had come out and said that his photographs had been misconstrued.

So not a single Haitian—despite trying to illegally rush the border of the United States—was ever whipped, or beaten, or even hit with a rein. Did anyone from the Biden administration issue any kind of apology for the lies they had spread? Did they reflect on how they had used these viral pieces of misinformation to convict several innocent law enforcement officers before the evidence in their case could even be reviewed by a panel of experts?

Of course not. This phony scandal was the administration's way to distract the public from the absolute disaster that was unfolding in Del Rio at the time, and paint Border Patrol agents as racist so they could continue their efforts to defame and defund them. Before the story about the Border Patrol "whipping migrants" broke, there were videos every day of the tens of thousands of people pouring into the city from Mexico. Now, if you were going to hear anything about the border and the influx of migrants coming in, part of the narrative would have to be also about those horrible Border Patrol agents. Just how Democrats wanted it to be.

Throughout the entire meltdown at the border, the Biden administration has treated public awareness as something to be discouraged and avoided. As Tom Homan, who led ICE under President Trump, pointed out in a piece for The Heritage Foundation, the Biden administration tried to block information from trickling out by instituting a federal ban on drone photography; many videos of the border disaster were obtained by Fox News reporter Bill Melugin using drones. But when it became clear that their drone ban was going to fail and the images were going to come out no matter what, Homan wrote, the administration "removed its drone ban and made up a new story: Border Patrol agents on horseback were whipping Haitian migrants."[26]

This story was always a distraction from the real problem: Our southern border is wide open. Our Border Patrol agents are overwhelmed. Despite their essential mission, they feel vilified and demoralized. Every day, the Biden administration seems to deliberately search for ways to make their job more difficult, and more hopeless. Suicides by Border Patrol agents are at an all-time high, with eight agents killing themselves in a single year and three in just a 15-day span last November.[27] The least we could do is be fully honest about the difficulties the Border Patrol face. Instead, the Biden administration rewards them only with lies.

These lies, though, only work with the support of an equally dishonest press. In an internal memo released March 2021, the Associated Press told its reporters and editors not to use the word "crisis" when reporting on the border. The editor who sent the memo referred to the "situation" at the border as something that "President Biden must deal with" rather than something he created due to his own incompetence. The memo then cautioned all reporters at the AP to avoid "charged language" when discussing the border.

Remember once again the Party's command in Orwell's *1984*: "Reject the evidence of your eyes and ears." Right now, Joe Biden and the liberals are telling you to reject what you can see right in front of your face. And if you refuse, they have tactics for dealing with you. If you *do* voice your concerns about the border, there are hundreds if not thousands of journalist Lee Harvey Oswalds ready to character-assassinate you.

Which brings me to the most troubling part of our border crisis.

A Formula for Disaster

Biden wasn't elected because he knew what he was doing. He wasn't even elected because of his many years of accomplishment-free service in the United States Senate.

No. Joe Biden was elected because he "cares." That, we were assured, was the good news about him. During the campaign, he never hesitated before leaning in close—often *too close*—to whisper in the ears of aggrieved people, or to promise that his administration was going to be one big nation-healing group hug. He just cared that much. And, hey, maybe he does care about some people . . . if they're from the right demographics.

In October of 2021, Biden's Food and Drug Administration was contacted by a whistleblower from a facility owned by Abbott Laboratories. This company, which became a household name for making quick, cheap Covid tests, also produces a large amount of the baby formula sold in the United States. At the time, one infant in Texas had already become ill with a foodborne pathogen that had worked its way into the formula at Abbott's facility in Sturgis, Michigan.

It was the FDA's job to investigate the issue, but it dragged its feet due to "Covid-19 related staffing issues."[28] Then, when the FDA finally attempted to plan a visit to the site of the contamination, they were again delayed because of a potential Covid outbreak at the plant (apparently, Biden's beloved vaccine wasn't enough to protect them). The FDA only managed to make its inspection in January, three months after the initial whistleblower complaint. In that time, two infants had died from tainted baby formula traced back to the plant. But hey, just imagine if somebody had gotten a bad cough by inspecting it earlier!

When the inspection was done and the report was written, the Abbott plant was shut down and this country's supply of baby formula began drying up. Soon, the shelves of supermarkets and pharmacies were empty. Signs went up letting new mothers know that it might be weeks and months before they could purchase any formula for their infants. Mothers across the country searched frantically through drug stores and supermarkets and corner shops for stray cases of formula, only to find the shelves bare. I myself felt like a baby formula dealer. My daughter had no formula for my grandson. Neither did a dear friend. No one knew where to go. We were all panicked. On my show *The Five*, I complained and asked viewers if they knew anywhere we could buy formula. A few emailed me and I followed up. I was getting something that was unobtainable, like a middleman buying and then delivering the goods to the designated infant.

But one place where the shelves were not empty was at the entry point of the southern border. Those mothers coming in by the hundreds of thousands had all the formula they needed. The federal government made sure of it.

According to Jen Psaki, there were pallets of baby formula down at the border because the administration needed to abide by the *Flores* decision, a court ruling that set certain standards for the treatment of young migrants. Of course, she never mentioned the fact that there wouldn't *be* quite so many children at the border if her boss had not promised open borders. She thumbed her nose at the parents who paid the taxes to purchase baby formula for illegals and ended up not finding any for their own American children.

It was Biden at his best. Take care of illegals, Americans come last.

When will this end? When is enough, enough? How many drug mules and cartel killers can we let through while still pretending America is the land entrusted to us by our ancestors? How many millions of people can our strained safety net afford? How long do our own shelves have to go empty for the sake of illegal arrivals before the public realizes their birthright has been given away to those who only see America as a meal ticket? How long can our own administration flagrantly ignore our own immigration laws before the public decides that *every* law is a joke? How many nighttime migrant flights can our cities sustain before America stops feeling like a sovereign nation and starts feeling like one overcrowded refugee camp with benefits?

The Marxist Aversion to Democracy

Cartoon Socialism

Do you remember "The Life of Julia"?

It sounds like one of those pretentious, Oscar-nominated films you hear about every December, but "The Life of Julia" was actually the name of a short online caricature President Barack Obama's PR team released back in May of 2012. A closer look at this revealed a cartoon that had as its underlying theme the total abandonment of the fundamental principles of this country.

Back in 2012 people still believed the Mayan calendar's prediction that the world would end, or that Barack Obama would still usher in an era of racial unity in America. It was truly a different time. So I'll understand if you've forgotten about Julia and her role in Obama's slideshow propaganda.

Obama's team created a cartoon slideshow about how life would be better for Julia under a second Obama term and ultimately under the Left's view of the takedown of America. "The Life of Julia" campaign was supposed to prove that Barack Obama's socialist, big-government ideology would be better for American children in the long run than the supposedly harsh, conservative ideas of his opponent, Mitt Romney. (Personally, I never liked Mitt—he lost me with the dog on top of his car—but I digress.)

Take a look at Julia's "life," and you'll see that everything the Left is doing now—mask mandates, speech codes, and an attempted takeover of our schools—has been part of their playbook for a long, long time. There is no decision in your life, however small, that they would not love to make for you. Give them a few years, and they'll start telling *you* what *your* pronouns are!

The Julia video was mocked by right-thinking Americans. And rightfully so. The video has long since been scrubbed from Barack Obama's website—you'll see why.

The first slide shows Julia as a young girl in a dress. She's playing with toys on the floor. Her parents are nowhere in sight.

The caption above this picture reads:

Under President Obama: Julia is enrolled in a Head Start program to help her get ready for school. Because of steps President Obama has taken to improve programs like this one, Julia joins thousands of students across the country who will start kindergarten ready to learn and succeed.

Under Mitt Romney: The Romney/Ryan budget could cut programs like Head Start by 20 percent, meaning the program would offer 200,000 fewer slots per year.[1]

In the next slide, Julia is standing next to her locker in a high school hallway. The caption says that Julia's high school "is part of the Race to the Top program, implemented by President Obama," while "the Romney/Ryan budget would cut funding for public education to pay for tax cuts for millionaires."

On and on it goes. An observant user clicking through this video might notice that at every stage of her life Julia is alone. She has no husband, no parents, and no extended family. Instead, she is supported by the federal government, which, in Obama's ideal future, is deeply involved in every aspect of her life. When she turns eighteen, she gets a Pell Grant to attend college. During her senior year, the government pays for a surgery and, a few years after this, she sues her employer under the Lilly Ledbetter Fair Pay Act to demand a raise.

Federal grants, taxpayer-funded surgeries, and employee lawsuits—the American Dream!

Everything in Julia's life, the ad suggests, will be taken care of by the government—her student loans, her birth control, and, eventually, her salary and retirement funds. This "success" provides Julia a lot of time to fulfill what the Left thinks life is really about: being alone in your apartment and "binge-watching" your favorite television shows (preferably Netflix shows produced by Barack Obama, who signed a deal with the streaming company in 2018).

But the most troubling slides come in the middle, when Julia, still alone, "decides to have a child." Over a picture of a pregnant Julia standing in a doctor's office, a caption notes that "throughout her pregnancy, she benefits from maternal checkups, prenatal care, and free screenings under healthcare reform." One slide later, she's standing at her mailbox with her son, Zachary—the only other human being who appears in the campaign—waiting for him to get on a school bus. Again, no father in sight.

The caption?

Under President Obama: Julia's son Zachary starts kinder-garten. The public schools in their neighborhood have bet-ter facilities and great teachers because of President Obama's investments in education and programs like Race to the Top.

The message was clear. With Zachary, the government-sponsored life begins anew. Under Barack Obama and the liberals, the govern-ment will replace the family unit. This government promises to take care of your healthcare, your job, and the education of your chil-dren. There are the government's promises (which they will break, of course) to take care of you like a beloved child, but with that also is the *guarantee* that they will make all your decisions and command absolute authority over you. The American Dream is no more. This is the antithesis of individual responsibility. It creates a government with a centric socialist program, the theme and the underpinning of this, where a welfare state will spend billions to guarantee its political and ideological base. Laying the groundwork for where we are now. The government has your back. And no longer needs you to com-pete or climb any ladder to succeed. You are their child.

All they will ask for up front is a huge share of your income in taxes—something that is never mentioned in the life of Julia—and the right to take your children into their classrooms, a place where they start the Marxist indoctrination where merit and initiative have no place, cementing the reliance on government programs. It would take years before American parents would rise up as they did in Virginia by electing Governor Youngkin who opposed the Left's belief that parents shouldn't be telling schools what they should teach after parents objected to critical race theory being propagated in their children's schools. President Biden proved his allegiance to this agenda in 2022 when he doubled down on the theme that children belonged to the schools.

When "The Life of Julia" hit the web in 2012, it was received poorly. Today we would say there were "memes" about it. It was clear that the Obama campaign had miscalculated. As it turns out, many young women weren't excited to learn that the Democrats saw them all as future isolated, welfare-dependent mothers who had to check with the federal government every time they had to so much as sneeze.

Writing in the *Wall Street Journal,* James Taranto pointed out that "nothing happens to Julia between 42 and 65. That period includes the typical peak earning years—the time at which, assuming Julia is gainfully employed, she will be paying the biggest price for 'Obama's' generosity . . . [the campaign] presents all of these benefits as 'free,' never acknowledging that they are paid for through coercive taxation."[2]

After a barrage of similar criticism, many of them written by the very women who were supposed to be convinced by the slideshow, the Obama campaign pulled the plug on cartoon Julia (it's unclear whether Julia's euthanization was covered by the government). For the next four years, we didn't hear from her. Although the Obama administration continued to push the big-government policies that were displayed in that ad campaign, they did not succeed in bringing their 'cartoon socialism' to the United States of America. What the Left learned was that they had to be more subtle and gradually reverse the fundamental tenets of this country. Their goal was to reverse the economic advances we had made and for them to turn us into a lazy government reliant society where there was no individual ambition. They had to be far more cunning and strategic without being so overt.

After four years of President Trump, who fought backward liberal policies for his entire term despite unprecedented obstruction from all sides, it seemed that we were further than ever from the gray bureaucratic state envisioned by the Obama campaign. Tax rates on middle-class families went down. In some schools (you may need to sit down before you read this) students were even taught to *love* America, and not to express pseudointellectual disdain for their country.

Then Biden showed up. His White House re-animated the lifeless, cartoon corpse of Julia, like an old Hollywood product getting a Netflix "reboot" . . . like the kind that Obama now produces.

The Afterlife of Julia

In April of 2022, President Joe Biden hosted a reception to honor Kurt Russell. Sadly, this was not Reagan-era action hero Kurt Russell, but another one. This other, terrible Kurt Russell was an educator from Ohio who'd been chosen as one of the Biden White House's "Teachers of the Year." Over the past few months, Russell had made headlines in his hometown of Oberlin for his willingness to teach high school students about "race, gender, and oppression."[3] In his classes, Russell encouraged students to discuss "the racism, sexism, and homophobia which they currently experience."[4]

Speaking in the East Room of the White House, Kurt Russell said he was "blessed to be a part of a profession that transforms and legitimizes student voices and plants the groundwork for a more culturally responsive education."[5]

Shortly afterward, Biden took to the microphone and congratulated Russell and the other teachers being honored that day—nearly all of whom were similarly woke—for helping their students "not only learn history but see—see what they—that they have a role in shaping history."

Then he delivered a line that should have sent a shiver down every parent's spine. "They're all our children," he said. "And the reason you're the Teacher of the Year is because you recognize that. They're not somebody else's children. They're like yours when they're in the classroom."[6]

I'm sorry, *what?* At the time Joe was speaking, there was a heated debate going on about what should and should not be taught in classrooms. When Covid-19 hit and the lockdowns began, children were forced to do their work from home, and parents finally got to see and hear exactly what nonsense had been getting foisted onto their children for years. They saw gender theory and Critical Race Theory. They saw flagrantly pornographic books about sexual discovery pushed onto young children in the guise of "sex education." Parents learned that white children were being forced to "admit their racism," while black children were being taught that behind every problem (from the climate in Africa to getting a flat tire) was a white face.

Put simply: the Covid lockdowns allowed parents to see, many for the first time, how schools were perverting, corrupting, and radicalizing their children. (To the credit of liberals, maybe *this* was the benefit to the school lockdowns that they always talked about?)

Parents were horrified, as they should have been, and they finally began speaking out.

And in the middle of all of it, Biden had the unmitigated gall to double down and tell parents that in school, students belong to the teachers.

This is classic Marxism.

Friedrich Engels was a close friend of Karl Marx and his coauthor on *The Communist Manifesto*. In the first draft of that sinister work,

Engels included a call for the abolition of the family unit by ending the dependence "of the wife upon the husband and of the children upon the parents." He called for building "common dwellings for communities of citizens" to replace the family home. Elsewhere, Engels wrote that one of the main "principles of Communism" would be the "Education of all children, from the moment they can leave their mother's care, in national establishments at national cost. Education and production together."[7] He and Marx wrote together that they wanted to get rid of the "hallowed co-relation of parent and child."

Take out the head and the body will follow. Communists know that the family is their great obstacle in their desire to indoctrinate and control people. Look for a common thread in their propaganda, and you will see they seek to undermine anyone who stands in the way of leftists being in charge (a reason why so many of them also hate God). For a long time, the Left has known that when you want to indoctrinate people with their radical ideas, it's best to do it before their brains are fully developed. As the poem says, "The hand that rocks the cradle is the hand that rules the world." That is why they always seek to undermine parents.

"Do you charge us with wanting to stop the exploitation of children by their parents?" Marx wrote. "To this crime we plead guilty. . . . The Communists have not invented the intervention of society in education; they do but seek to alter the character of that intervention."[8]

So the Left wants to "alter the character" of their intervention in the lives of our children. Interesting. Suddenly, that line from Biden's "Teacher of the Year" about wanting to "transform student voices" doesn't seem so innocent, does it?

Of course, Marxism didn't end when Karl Marx died in 1883. As an ideology, it was just getting started. He had plenty of disciples, and they've been spreading his ideas around the world for a century and a half now. Throughout recent history, several countries have attempted to take these left-wing ideas and build societies around them. It has never gone well. In Russia, after the Revolution of 1917, the avowed Marxist Leonid Sabsovich worked on behalf of the Kremlin to build "children's towns," where parents would send their children to live and be educated by the state. Sabsovich stressed that these towns should be built "at a distance from the family." He argued, according to a recent study of his work, "for a total separation of children from parents starting in the earliest years of child development."[9]

The same thing happened in Hungary, where the communists had a brief shot at leadership beginning in 1919. There, another genius named Georg Lukacs designed a school system that would, in the words of his biographer, "destroy the family." As Hungary's culture and education commissar, Lukacs sought to instruct children in a way that would bring about a complete takedown of the country's established order. The first step, he knew, was to change the way that children were taught to think about politics, religion, and most importantly, their families.

According to a biography cited by Mike Gonzalez in a piece for The Heritage Foundation, the school system that resulted from these ambitions was strange, to say the least:

> Special lectures were organized in schools and literature printed and distributed to 'instruct' children about free love, about the nature of sexual intercourse, about the archaic nature of bourgeois family codes, about the outdatedness of monogamy, and the irrelevance of religion, which deprives man of all pleasure. Children urged thus to reject and deride

paternal authority and the authority of the church, and to ignore precepts of morality.[10]

Eventually, every society that adopted Marxist tactics such as these failed. The takedown of these countries succeeded, just not in the way the Marxists wanted. Everything fell apart. Economies crashed. Famines killed millions. But Marxism didn't just economically fail: on a personal level it created miserable families.

Anyone who's read even a few pages of history about socialist societies should be able to tell that Marxism is poison. Every country that's even tried to put the ideas of Marx and his disciples into practice has quickly fallen into ruin.

In most cases, children have fared the worst.

But do you know who *didn't* think Marxism was all that bad?

Barack Obama.

As a teenager, Obama was mentored by Franklin Marshall Davis, an older man who was described in 2015 as a "'hard-core member' of the Communist Party" by the *Washington Post*.[11] According to Paul Kengor, who wrote a book about Obama and Davis titled *The Communist*, Davis was "a lasting, permanent influence, an integral part of Obama's sojourn."[12] The two of them would sit up for hours with Obama's grandfather, a left-wing radical who brought him over to Davis's house to receive the kind of indoctrination he couldn't get in school.

In his doorstop of a memoir titled *A Promised Land*, Obama admits that he often read Marx in college so that he could pick up girls in his dorm buildings.

"Looking back," he writes, "it's embarrassing to recognize the degree to which my intellectual curiosity those first two years of college paralleled the interests of various women I was attempting to get to know: Marx and Marcuse so I had something to say to the long-legged socialist who lived in my dorm. Fanon and Gwendolyn Brooks for the smooth-skinned sociology major who never gave me a second look; Foucault and Woolf for the ethereal bisexual who wore mostly black."[13]

Do those names sound innocent? Boring? They're neither. Marcuse refers to Herbert Marcuse, the German philosopher who became a professor in America at Brandeis and UC San Diego, and who was, according to his pupil Paul Gottfried, a Stalinist. Fanon refers to the avowed Marxist Frantz Fanon, who pioneered the "postcolonial theory" that undergirds much of the later "woke" movement. Fanon believed that the West was "fundamentally racist," and that it needed to be overthrown by violent means. The "Foucault" with whom Obama was so enamored in college refers to Michel Foucault, another Marxist who believed Western traditions needed to be razed and rebuilt from the ground up. During a stay in Tunisia in 1968, Foucault abused several prepubescent children, a crime for which he was given a pass for several decades by the modern Left.

You'll notice by now that the abuse and perversion of children at the hands of leftists is a common theme. Perhaps not coincidentally, Michel Foucault and dozens of other left-wing intellectuals signed a petition in France in 1977 against the existence of age of consent laws.

If you've ever wondered where the insane ideas of Barack Obama—and, by extension, the ideas of most of the modern Democratic party—come from, now you know. Then, when it came time for Barack Obama to rule the country he learned to hate during his youth, he instituted policies that laid the groundwork for the takedown of America. During his time in office, taxes went up. The government began showing that it was willing to assert control over our freedom of speech. And more and more elements of our daily lives were given over to the government, all of it paid for by taxes on ordinary Americans. One of Obama's key policies during his first term was free college for all, an enormous expense that comes right out of the communist playbook.

Is anyone surprised when the Obama campaign had the chance to pitch itself to American voters after that disastrous first term, they designed a fake single woman named Julia who relied on the government for her every need? Karl Marx and his cronies would have been proud.

Of course, the American public rejected Julia and the Obama administration's vision for her life. While he did manage to win a second term, the government-takeover-of-everything plan slid into the background for a few years, then disappeared completely during the presidency of President Trump.

When Joe Biden showed up, the American people didn't want the extreme left-wing policies that Democrats had pushed a decade before. So did they work harder to craft policies that were good for all Americans? Did they ditch the wokeness and move to the center on key issues?

I'll answer for those in the back of the class: no.

Rather than simply announcing they want to enroll all children in Head Start programs on the American taxpayers' dime, the Biden team announced in its "American Family Plan" that "many children, but especially children of color and low-income children, do not have access to the full range of high-quality preschool programs available to their more affluent peers. . . . President Biden is calling for a national partnership with states to offer free, high-quality, accessible, and inclusive preschool to all three-and-four-year-olds."[14]

THE MARXIST AVERSION TO DEMOCRACY

Rather than simply stating that we need education programs like Race to the Top, we get this:

President Biden is calling on Congress to invest $9 billion in American teachers, addressing shortages, improving training and supports for teachers, and boosting teacher diversity. These investments will improve the quality of new teachers entering the profession, increase retention rates and increase the number of teachers of color, all of which will improve student outcomes.[15]

Rather than just give out tax cuts and Pell Grants to all students who want free college, Biden called for "$62 billion to invest in evidence-based strategies to strengthen completion and retention rates at community colleges and institutions that serve students from our most disadvantaged communities. This is alongside a $46 billion investment in Historically Black Colleges and Universities, TCUs, and MSIs."

What was going on? All Biden did was take the original Life-of-Julia recipe, shake it up, and add a dollop of Critical Race Theory. That's become the guiding impulse in almost every part of Biden's education policy, from preschool to grad school. It guides where we spend money, of course, but even more sinisterly, it dictates what is taught in the classroom. Instead of pursuing what is best for all Americans, every policy is framed as a way to elevate certain preferred groups and hold down or punish certain other ones (okay, you know which one I mean: ordinary white people).

The Liberal Playbook: Young Reader's Edition

Last year, in Buffalo, New York, students in kindergarten classrooms all over the city sat down to watch a video during their morning lessons. This video was created by an anonymous person on YouTube, and according to the Buffalo School District, it was mandatory for every five-year-old in the city to watch it.

In the first few seconds, a group of cartoon black children come across the screen. They say that they are dead, and that they've been killed by "racist police and state-sanctioned violence."[16] By the end of the video, these children in Buffalo—most of whom lack the ability to read full words without help—are taught to believe that in the United States of America, a common cause of death for black five-year-olds is murder by police.

This is a lie, plain and simple.

But it's a lie that has worked its way into the classrooms of Buffalo thanks to an education administrator named Fatima Morrell, a devoted Marxist who believes the school district should be remade according to "woke" principles.[17] According to reporting by the independent journalist Christopher Rufo, whose work has done more than anyone else to introduce Critical Race Theory to the American public, the curriculum that Morrel designed says that America is "built on racism," and that all Americans are guilty of "implicit racial bias."

In Morrell's version of fifth grade, children are told that there is a "school-to-grave pipeline" for black students, and that American society was designed for "the impoverishment of people of color and enrichment of white people."[18] They learn that the United States "created a social system that had racist economic inequality built into its foundation," and that "the [current] wealth gap is the result of black slavery, which created unjust wealth for white people," who are "unfairly rich."

The brainwashing continues throughout high school, where, according to Rufo's reporting, children are taught that white people—and only white people—have "created a 'retributive,' 'merit-based' justice system, which relies on harsh punishment and creates inequalities. Traditional Africans, on the other hand, relied on a 'restorative,' 'needs-based' justice system focused on healing, giving to each according to his need, and prioritizing 'collective value' over individual rights."[19]

This is how you enact a takedown of America—not by waving pitchforks or throwing bricks through windows (although that certainly helps), but by teaching children that the country is rotten and evil, and that anyone who seeks to destroy it is doing us all a favor.

All over the country, teachers, many of whom have been trained in Marxist education theory at graduate schools of education, are spreading lies, while the ones who aren't already eager to do so, are pressured to join in by leftist administrators.

In Seattle, shortly after the George Floyd riots, teachers were told during a training session that they must teach that white people were guilty of "spirit murder" against black students. This, according to the Marxist psychos running the session, means that American schools "murder the souls of Black children every day through systemic, institutionalized, anti-Black, state-sanctioned violence."[20]

Again, like so much Marxism, this is an attempt to justify their own hatred and violence. What they are saying is that if alleged victims (in this example the Left uses black students) are already experiencing violence ("spiritual murder") then that, in their minds, justifies very real violence toward their "oppressors."

In California, according to the Center for Renewing America, third-grade students "were made to deconstruct" their racial identity and rank themselves according to their 'power and privilege' in school."[21] In Philadelphia, teachers were encouraged to attend a workshop that showed them how to teach children about transgender surgeries, masturbation, and "kinks." Around the same time, Los Angeles children were made to sort themselves into groups based on their skin color and racial identity.

Then there's the reading material. Just one look at the titles is enough to let you know that something has been wrong in the classrooms of our nation for a long time. Do these people really expect us to stand by while our kids cozy up with the latest edition of *Gender Queer*, which depicts explicit sex acts and contains discussions on masturbation? Or *Lawn Boy*, which describes two fourth-grade boys having oral sex?

If you've ever wondered what kinds of people believe we should be pushing this crap to our children, all you have to do is perform a quick internet search. It seems that lately, the only thing these people like more than indoctrinating our children is bragging about it on the internet.

Consider, for instance, the teacher who posted on TikTok about how she took down the American flag in her room because it "made her uncomfortable" and replaced it with the LGBTQ pride flag, making all the kids in her class pledge allegiance to *that* instead. Or the one who screamed "TURN OFF THE FOX NEWS" at her students. Then, of course, there is the teacher who described the curriculum of her preschool class this way: "We have been talking about gender, skin color, consent, empathy, our bodies, and autonomy—it has been *fabulous*!"[22] Preschoolers!

Sadly, I am not even scratching the surface.

If you ever need your daily fix of this insanity, head over to the Twitter account LibsofTikTok (if they haven't found a way to ban it by the time you read this), which collects and curates these videos. You'll be amazed at just how far the woke virus was able to spread through our schools—and, sadly, through our society in general—while no one was looking.

CRT and radical gender ideology go great with any liberal policy, because it makes criticizing those policies somehow "racist," or "transphobic," and it cows members of the public into shutting up. It also emboldens the people pushing the policy itself. The shield of Critical Race Theory lets woke radicals pretend that the deranged policies imaginable are a perfectly acceptable weapon of "antiracism," and makes them confident they can do it all right in the open. Any parents who disagree, they believe, will be so afraid of getting called racists that they'll just sit down and shut up.

Don't believe me? Consider this: During a gubernatorial debate in Virginia, liberal candidate Terry McAuliffe proudly boasted that he was kicking parents *out* of the classroom.

"I'm not going to let parents come into schools and actually take books out and make their own decisions," he said. "I don't think parents should be telling schools what to teach."[23] The imprimatur of Critical Race Theory and gender wokeness made him feel empowered to identify parents themselves as the enemy.

This debate, mind you, came amid a vitriolic fight between parents and teachers in Virginia and elsewhere in the United States. During the pandemic, parents had looked over the shoulders of their children, and been shocked by lessons in pornography and "white guilt" on their children's laptops and iPads. They saw their kids being assigned "children's versions" of core anti-white CRT texts by Ibram X. Kendi or Nikole Hannah-Jones, who teach that America is founded on the principles of white supremacy and racism.

And so, they spoke up. None of these parents protesting, to my knowledge, said these books shouldn't exist, or that their publishers had no right to sell them for money to willing buyers.

These parents only suggested that maybe, just *maybe*, kids should learn the alphabet before being taught everything is the white man's fault. They believed it was probably a bad idea to line up children and have them do "privilege walks" on the playground instead of just reading good, old-fashioned history textbooks, or knowing their multiplication tables. And for that, they were treated as the enemies of education. Some of them were even treated as if they were criminals.

That's exactly what happened in June of 2021.

Loudoun County

On the evening of June 22, in Loudoun County, Virginia, a plumber named Scott Smith showed up at a school board meeting, mad as hell and unable to take it anymore. Scott, however, would have to wait to speak as there was something of a line of angry parents— more than 250 in total. Due to the back-and-forth fighting between parents and teachers that had been going on in Loudoun County for the better part of two years (Critical Race Theory, sexual education in classrooms, school closings, etc. etc.), the number of pissed-off parents looking to speak their minds was long.

Scott Smith sat down in the audience with his wife and waited patiently for his turn—more than I would have been able to do.

A little over a month earlier, Smith's daughter had been sexually assaulted in a high school girls' bathroom. The perpetrator was a biologically male student wearing a dress. Amazingly, this student was allowed to be in the girls' bathroom because the school was trying out a new policy that would allow students to "use the bathroom that best conforms with the gender of their choice."

Several parents had raised concerns that adopting such a policy in bathrooms and locker rooms would result in the sexual assault of actual women. These people were called bigots by the school board, and told to sit down and shut up.

On the day his daughter was sexually assaulted, Scott Smith was called into the principal's office of her school. He was told only that his daughter was "attacked" by another student. He did not learn until he pressed for details that the assailant was transgender, or that the attack was sexual. After questioning the principal, Smith also learned the school would not be referring this heinous crime to the police.

When he heard this, Smith, quite understandably, began raising his voice and gesturing.

Eventually, according to an investigative report conducted months later by the *Daily Wire,* the police were called to Stone Bridge High School that day. But not to finally arrest the boy who sexually assaulted Scott Smith's daughter. Instead, the police were called *on Scott Smith* because he was *making a scene.*

By the time he arrived at the Loudoun County School Board meeting in June, Smith was at the end of his rope. His family had been let down by the people who were supposed to protect them. The school system had failed Smith's daughter by not protecting her from a predator, then dealt her a second indignity by refusing to hold her attacker accountable.

I'm sure Smith had a hard time holding his composure as the left-leaning ideologues on the school board debated the merits of Policy 8040, which would have made it mandatory for schools to allow all students to use whatever bathrooms "best aligned with their gender identities." When the issue of potential assaults in girls' bathrooms was raised—the very thing that had happened to Smith's daughter—one of the school board members waved it off.

"I think it's important to keep our perspective on this," he said. "We've heard it several times tonight from our public speakers. But the predator transgender student or person simply does not exist."[24]

This was a lie, plain and simple, and Scott Smith knew it. Unfortunately, he never got the chance to speak. A few minutes into the meeting, a group of parents at the back of the room erupted into applause. One of the school board members, who believed applause was triggering and had requested the use of "jazz hands" instead, shut the whole thing down.

In America, the lunatics don't just run the asylums—we now let them run our schools.

A few parents went to the back of the room to continue giving their speeches, and Scott Smith and his wife were among them. A few minutes into this makeshift demonstration, they were approached by a woman from the neighborhood. According to the account in the *Daily Wire*, this woman asked why they had come to the meeting. Smith's wife, who thought this woman was a friend, told her everything—the attack, the cover-up, and the various ways he had been mistreated by the school board.

When the woman looked Smith in the eyes and said, calmly, "That's not what happened," something in him broke. He raised his voice.

Then, in a split second, he was on the ground. A police officer had tackled him.

His wife, watching the whole thing happen in horror, screamed, "This is what happens! My daughter was raped in school, and this is what happens!"

For the next few days, images of Scott Smith with his bare stomach hanging out and his hands cuffed behind his back began circulating online. The next day, they were on the covers of newspapers and home pages of websites. Shortly afterward, video footage of the incident was playing on cable news networks and commentators were warning about the "dangerous parents" who were coming to school board meetings intent on committing violent acts and intimidating board members into submission.

Shortly after the incident with Scott Smith occurred, the National Association of School Boards wrote a letter to the Biden administration claiming that "America's public schools and its education leaders [were] under an immediate threat."[25] They asked for assistance from federal law enforcement to deal with a "growing number of threats of violence and acts of intimidation occurring across the nation." As evidence, they cited twenty incidents that had occurred at school board meetings across the country. One of them was the incident with Scott Smith, though the letter didn't mention it was the police who tackled Smith for the crime of having a conversation.

Toward the end of the memo, the authors suggested using the Patriot Act, a Bush-era law designed for fighting terrorism, to go after parents who speak out at school board meetings. These people were, in effect, labeling parents who advocated for their children as potential domestic terrorists.

Less than a week later, Attorney General Merrick Garland responded by sending a memo to the FBI and other officials at the Department of Justice. Parroting the talking points he'd been given by the National Association of School Boards, he warned of a "disturbing spike in harassment, intimidation, and threats of violence against school administrators, board members, teachers, and staff who participate in the vital work of running our nation's public schools."[26] He instructed the FBI to look into the matter, once again treating parents like domestic terrorists. But there was more to be concerned about than the content of the memo.

The United States Justice Department and the FBI were being weaponized to go after parents concerned about their children. That technique has been used only by the most backward, authoritarian regimes in history. But the Biden administration, despite all its bluster about the other side being "fascist," decided that it would have no problem using federal law enforcement to intimidate parents into silence.

You might think, from their hysterical reaction to parents trying to control what books their children are assigned in school, that the Left simply hates the idea of "banning books." That's certainly how the Left would present themselves. But it's another lie. The Left attempts to ban books all the time. When it comes to removing literature, the Left doesn't just say that children shouldn't read these books, or that these books don't belong in the curricula of elementary schools. They say that these books should not exist, that any store that sells them should face boycotts, and that anyone who reads—or, God forbid, enjoys—them is somehow morally corrupt. The Left was engaging in Freudian projection all along: *they're* the ones who love banning books.

When the Left found out that Target was still selling copies of *Irreversible Damage,* the journalist Abigail Shrier's book on the horrific effects that transgender surgeries have on children, they threw a fit. Boycotts were threatened. Accusations of "transphobia" and "white supremacy" flew all over the internet.

Unable to stand up to the pressure, and probably remembering from 2020 how liberals defended the criminals who looted and burned down their stores, Target pulled the book from its shelves.

Do you think our schools would ever showcase Abigail Shrier's book about the horrors of transgender surgeries during the next "Banned Books Week"? Of course not. Like so much of the Left, its Banned Books Week is phony.

Unlike these liberal activists, conservative parents have merely demanded the power to decide how and when their children are taught about sensitive topics such as sex and gender identity. Some elected officials—the ones who aren't afraid to face down the Left— have listened. In the spring of 2022, Governor Ron DeSantis of Florida signed the Parental Rights in Education law, which prevents teachers from instructing students about gender identity or sexual matters between kindergarten and third grade. (In my opinion, DeSantis should've called it the No Pervert Talk law.)

Again, how could anyone possibly disagree with what DeSantis passed? Are there people who think that children in first grade really need to learn about sex and why some grown men like to wear dresses and makeup? If so, I'd like to know where they are right now to make sure it's at least one hundred yards from a school.

The bottom line is that liberals do not have a right to share their fetishes and sexual fantasies with our children. Believe it or not, "pervert talks" are not even something guaranteed in the Bill of Rights.

But in response to this very sensible law and a few others just like it, the liberals went nuts. Access to other people's children—who, as I've shown, they don't believe belong to their parents—is profoundly important to them.

Shortly after Ron DeSantis signed his bill, Randi Weingarten, the president of the American Federation of Teachers, called those parents "vocal minorities [who] want to marginalize LGBTQ kids, censor teachers, and ban books."[27] Asked about the efforts to remove certain books from the classrooms of our children,

Weingarten said, "We've been very lucky in America, and we in some ways live in a bubble for a long time. This is propaganda. This is misinformation. This is the way in which wars start. This is the way in which hatred starts."

"The way in which wars start?" Randi Weingarten believes that such things as privately encouraging other people's children to get sex change operations, is something worth going to *war over*?

She also uses that "misinformation" word again! Have you ever realized that whenever they throw that one out, they're never specific about where, exactly, the misinformation is coming from? Mostly, they just repeat it as many times as they can, throw out accusations of "racism," and hope that'll be enough.

Sometimes, they take us into tinfoil hat country.

Take MSNBC's Nicolle Wallace, who compared DeSantis's bill to the "dehumanization tactics" used in war.

"Russians," she said, "get the soldiers to rape children by dehumanizing them. Dehumanization as a practice is a tactic from war. It's being deployed in our politics. And people like you and I sometimes lose the plot. . . . But even the analysis loses sight of what this speech brings us back which is dehumanization has a cost right now."[28]

What? If you don't support teachers giving children lessons on sexuality and Critical Race Theory, then you're supposedly like a member of the Russian Army *raping children?* Such rhetoric is indefensible and insane, but in another way it's very valuable: it shows just how important it is for the Left to have unfettered access to, and control of, our children.

We need more people to have the courage of Scott Smith, and to speak up and not care if all hell breaks loose if it means exposing what goes on. Such bravery in defending your family from government tyranny is one of the only things keeping propaganda such as "The Life of Julia" a work of dystopian cartoon socialism.

The Marxist-inspired attacks on the family are just starting to bloom. Whether in schools where they secretly seek delve into all aspects of your child's sexuality including gender identity, or arresting fathers who seek answers after their daughter's rape. They threaten the complete destruction of another pillar of America.

Gaslighting

On his first day in the Oval Office, Joe Biden committed one of the ultimate crimes against America. He began the elimination of America's energy independence. That move literally destroyed the livelihood of countless Americans who were simply told to find new jobs in the green energy sector. It also put America in the subservient position of begging Venezuela and Saudi Arabia to provide oil for our very survival. To turn a nation that was a net exporter of energy to one dependent on foreign nations clearly not our allies required a great deal of gaslighting.

Gaslighting is deceitfulness where one stubbornly insists that something is the case, when it's just the opposite. The intent is to make you think you're crazy. When the Left invited riots throughout the summer of 2020, and then later says there wasn't widespread rioting and the protests were "peaceful," that was gaslighting. When violent rioters attacked police and created chaos in American cities and then said the resulting murder wave was the result of "Covid," that's gaslighting. Get the drift? It's a way of making you feel like you're losing your grip on reality, but that's because they are denying reality.

And when it comes to America's energy independence, we are being gaslit. Biden and his progressive wackos insist on abandoning America's energy independence on the theory that fossil fuels are an existential threat endangering all of us. They insist we now abandon the policies that made us energy independent in the first place: such as investment in fossil fuels and high levels of drilling.

A House on Fire

The gaslighting started in January of 2019. An unbalanced teenager named Greta Thunberg took a few days off from school and headed to The World Economic Forum in Davos, Switzerland, where, "leaders from business, government, international organizations, civil society, and academia come together to address critical issues at the start of each year."[1] Translation: the meeting is another venue for liberal elites who fly in on their fuel-guzzling private jets, get together, collude on ways to gain even more power and make even more money, but then pretend that the last thing on anyone's mind is power and money. They want us to believe they were only meeting to discuss climate change and other "global problems." It's the rich throwing themselves a party but acting like they're saving the world.

Think of it as the Oscars, minus one Will Smith slap.

That year at Davos, the star of the show was the aforementioned Greta, a sixteen-year-old who had made a name for herself as a climate activist in her home country of Sweden. Greta's father is an actor; her mother is an opera singer and the country's 2009 Eurovision representative. Since show business and reality TV run in Greta's family, it might explain her need for attention.

By 2019, Greta had already been a rising star for several years, marked by the Radical Left as the movement's next big hero. She had given all kinds of speeches, almost always delivered as though she was auditioning to play one of the twin girls in *The Shining*. The core idea: we're all going to die very soon if we don't begin to take climate change seriously.

Toward the end of 2019, Greta accused every member of the United Nations of "stealing her dreams and her childhood" for not freaking out more about the changing climate. She demanded that governments adopt renewable energy technologies, and that they give up fossil fuels if they wanted to live out their days without catching fire every time they step outside.

But it was her speech in Davos, delivered just a few weeks into the new year, that really put this *Sweden's Got Talent* star on the map. During her address, Greta said "Our house is on fire." She said we were, "less than twelve years away from not being able to undo our mistakes."[2]

That number was wildly exaggerated and based on scientific modeling of the "Al Gore promised Manhattan would be underwater by 2016" sort. Alexandria Ocasio-Cortez—another genius whose political career was essentially started via a casting call—would use the same study Greta used to claim, falsely, that "The world is going to end in twelve years if we don't address climate change."[3] Given that this was four years ago, and that AOC is still living comfortably in New York (a city she presumably believes will soon be underwater), I think we can safely assume that something is *very* wrong with the numbers she's citing. It's not that AOC does not know her numbers are wrong. It's more likely she doesn't care.

For the Left, the maxim is "Just because something is a lie, doesn't mean it's not *true*." As Elon Musk says: let that sink in.

Toward the end of her speech, Greta gave us all an order—one that world leaders, much to the detriment of their people, would soon heed.

"Adults keep saying: 'We owe it to the young people to give them hope,'" Greta said. "But I don't want your hope. I don't want you to be hopeful. I want you to panic. I want you to feel the fear I feel every day. And then I want you to act."[4]

Sadly, the world took Greta's song to heart. And they listened largely because of a coordinated campaign by the American liberal media to take Greta—who, according to some, seems to suffer from some deep social and psychological stresses—and turn her into a prophet, an expert, and a martyr all at once. Not until Saint Anthony Fauci posed for the cover of *InStyle* magazine, in his *Miami Vice* sunglasses, would such praise be heaped on someone so unqualified and undeserving. Notice another theme here: when it comes to their political causes, the Radical Left is willing to use anyone, even children.

Satirist and free speech activist Konstantin Kisin didn't take Greta seriously as noted in his lecture to the woke culture at Oxford:

> For tonight, and tonight only, I will join you. I will join you in worshiping at the feet of Saint Greta of climate change. Let us all accept right here that we are living through a climate emergency and our stocks of polar bears are running extremely low. I join you it this view. I truly do. Now, what are we to do about this huge problem facing humanity. What can we in Britain do? We can only do one thing. Do you know why? This country is responsible for 2% of global carbon emissions, which means that if Britain were to sink into the sea right now, it would make absolutely no

difference to the issue of climate change. Do you know why? Because the future of the climate is going to be decided in Asia and in Latin America.[5]

Kisin ended by calling on climate activists to end their worship of Greta and the protest culture and instead get a real job.

For the next three years, the world, however, took Greta's advice and did a whole lot of panicking. Spurred on by global supervillains like Klaus Schwab—the founder of the World Economic Forum, which puts the Davos conference together every year—the leaders of several major companies and countries doubled down on their commitments to renewable energy technology.

Schwab's home country of Germany had plowed billions of dollars into wind farms in a bid to wean themselves off coal, oil, and natural gas. Meanwhile, the government shut down several power plants that had provided cheap, reliable energy for years. They were part of the Global Reset who wanted fossil fuels gone.

In 2018, the German government announced that it wasn't going to meet its goals. They were forced to admit that even with record investment in renewable energy, their carbon emissions hadn't gone down at all since roughly 2009. Later that year, they announced plans to "bulldoze an ancient church and forest in order to get to the coal underneath it," acknowledging that the country now faced an energy emergency.[6]

Unfortunately, it wasn't just Germany. In July of 2021, the European Commission—the main governing body of the European Union—unveiled the world's most ambitious program ever to eliminate fossil fuels for the sake of the climate. Their ambitious goals included slashing greenhouse gasses to 55% of 1990 levels by 2030. Just like John F. Kennedy's pledge to land a man on the moon by

1970, the Europeans were boldly promising to reach a difficult goal in less than a decade . . . except instead of sending man to the stars, they were sending him back to the Stone Age.

Within months there were signs of a crisis—not a dramatic rise in sea levels or a catastrophic heat wave, but an energy crisis unlike anything the world had seen in centuries. An Associated Press report described the disaster:

> Power shortages are turning out streetlights and shutting down factories in China. The poor in Brazil are choosing between paying for food or electricity. German corn and wheat farmers can't find fertilizer, made using natural gas. And fears are rising that Europe will have to ration electricity if it's a cold winter.[7]

When reading liberal newspapers, it's a good habit to notice how they sometimes insert politically incorrect facts, the real meat of the story, at the end. In this case, at the bottom were a few of the reasons the global energy market was suddenly in tatters. Unsurprisingly, at number one was the increase in demand after the end of Covid lockdowns. But then, just after that, was this sentence: "A cold winter depleted reserves, then the summer was less windy than usual, so wind turbines didn't generate as much energy as expected."

Like treasure buried at the bottom of the ocean, there at the end of the reporting was the real cause of the problem.

At least in Russia citizens did not have these problems. While European governments were busy trying to keep the temperature of the globe from rising a single degree, the Russian government was doubling down on its control of oil markets. Joe Biden had done his part to contribute to Russia's energy independence by giving Russia a Nord Stream 2 gas pipeline waiver which was totally inconsistent with his alleged concern for the environment and ultimately was leverage that weakened European states by increasing dependency on Moscow.[8] That waiver helped give Russia the ability to invade Ukraine. Already the largest supplier of oil and natural gas in the region, Europe's war on carbon only increased Russia's power over European countries. In the aftermath of Putin's invasion of Ukraine, the Russian government has exercised that power, cutting off exports and watching the people of Europe panic.

The countries of Europe are now suffering under Putin's boot, who controls nearly all access to cheap, usable energy in the region. And they have done it to themselves by believing fossil fuels were an existential threat to our existence.

California

The energy-crazed leftists have taken root in the liberal state of California. The embrace of that environmentalist lunacy is fueled by a Democrat governor with slicked-back hair and a flair for virtue signaling who sees himself catapulted to the White House (maybe by windmills) on these leftist issues.

In 2020 Governor Gavin Newsom signed legislation to ban the sale of gas-powered cars by the year 2035.[9] If that feels impossibly far into the future, it's not. When he did, Newsom committed California to a gas-free future, but also lines of car-owners stretching for blocks looking to charge those electric vehicles because of an electric grid that couldn't keep up. The electric grid, in fact, was on the verge of short circuiting thanks to California's increasing dependence on unreliable, inefficient "clean" energy sources. That didn't bother Newsom in the least. His plan was to force citizens to buy electric cars and later tell those same people their cars cannot charge because there wasn't enough wind that year to power the state's electric grid. When that happens, liberals will have people exactly where they want them: locked in their homes, unable to go anywhere.

According to Newsom, you can keep your dead electric car in your driveway and homeless drug addicts on the streets, but he can't promise you that you'll be able to stay warm. California voted to ban the sale of all-natural gas-fired space heaters and water heating appliances by 2030. Don't be shocked if they're coming for your gas stove, not just in California but in New York. They don't care that virtually every famous chef cooks on a gas stove including a not-so-famous chef—me. Get a vent and call it a day. And further out on the horizon, another deadline is approaching: by 2045, California wants to be at 100% renewable, zero-carbon electricity generation.[10]

In parts of dry California, people already pray for it to rain. Because of Governor Gavin Newsom's environmental policies, now they need to pray for wind too.

The only way California, and the rest of the country for that matter, can move toward zero carbon-based electricity is to sabotage electric output. This is going to hurt people for no reason other than zealots wanting to feel like they have power. The totalitarian instinct of those on the Left regardless of the issue is to dictate to the rest of us. They call it "making a difference." Even though that difference may have a negligible or even negative impact on the climate or anything else, and could be ruining your life, it makes them feel important.

The ones who insist we eradicate the use of fossil fuels condemn nuclear energy, which has been proven over the years to be the cleanest, most efficient form of energy in human history.

Rarely do you hear about natural gas by these alarmists. Probably because it is considered a fossil fuel. According to an IGS Energy report however, "natural gas has a 92% efficiency rate from wellhead to home compared to electricity generated by coal, which operates at only a 32% efficiency rate."[11] It is one of our greatest domestic energy sources. If Gavin Newsom were really serious about cutting California's carbon emissions to zero by 2045, then the first and best step would be going all-in on nuclear power. Instead, California is desperately trying to *get rid* of the nuclear power it already has. California has just one nuclear plant left, at Diablo Canyon, just north of Los Angeles. In 2018, California regulators approved a plan to shut the plant down by 2025. Now, as California's power grid crumbles, lawmakers have belatedly realized that disabling the single most-reliable source of power in their state might be a bad idea. So they've decided to stop the plant's closure . . . for another five years.

Why does the Left hate nuclear so much? My theory is that it's because it's a technology that already exists and would completely solve the problems they have spent so long complaining about. In short, going nuclear (literally) would not give them the power and self-satisfaction of changing our behavior and rationing our energy to their whims. Put another way, the Left hates nuclear because it works, and would help preserve our hard-won civilization. The Left, meanwhile, is always nursing the subconscious desire to sweep civilization away, forever.

As he went about trying to undo the Industrial Revolution, Newsom simultaneously filmed a campaign ad encouraging Floridians to move to California. Floridians, he said, were being oppressed by Republican leaders who were "banning books, making it harder to vote, restricting speech in classrooms, and criminalizing women and doctors."

It would take a separate book to truly untangle all the lies and deceitful implications in Newsom's sentence. Almost every word was a lie. Governor Newsom added, without a hint of irony, "Move to California, where we still believe in freedom."

Not the freedom to drive the car you want, of course. Or to use a gas stove in your new home. Or to carry a gun to protect yourself. True freedom belongs to the criminal repeatedly given the opportunity to reoffend, the druggie given the freedom to shoot up in open areas, and the homeless to camp out, fornicate, and relieve themselves anywhere they choose.

China Gets Away with It

China's world-leading pollution levels are of little concern to the green energy gang. Well, actually they matter when they're a way to *further* weaken our own country.

We already know Joe has been happy to give away America's wealth to anybody willing to walk in through Mexico. When Joe realized that some might not be willing to make that trip, he figured out how he could give away our money to those lazy ones. So in 2022, Biden signed onto a United Nations-backed fund to developing countries supposedly affected by "climate change." The nations that will benefit from these funds are in Asia, Africa, and Latin America. Biden agreed to give one billion dollars to developing countries to tackle climate change.[12] While Americans struggle with heating bills and fuel, Biden is cutting checks to help developing countries tackle global warming on the pretense that we are somehow responsible.

Now here's where the irony kicks in. The world's single biggest polluter, Communist China, is also eligible for these handouts. To add insult to injury, China got away with donating nothing itself to the global fund in spite of the fact that they are the world's leading polluter. As you read this, China is building scores of coal plants to power factories to build lithium batteries for the electric car you will be forced to buy.

The Trojan Horse Reveals Himself

Of course, none of the environmental insanity happening in America right now would be possible without the ultimate Trojan Horse Joe Biden, the man who opened his flanks to let out the environmental crazies.

But it was supposed to be different just a few years ago. Assuming Doc Brown's DeLorean from *Back to the Future* is still allowed to run on fossil fuels, let's use it to take a short trip back in time . . .

When Biden was running for president, he promised us that he was a moderate. That he alone could hold back the wave of Bernie Sanders socialists and pink-haired Elizabeth Warren voters who threatened the country.

Most of us wanted to believe he would be that moderate, but Biden is proof that sometimes no suit is more dangerous than an empty one.

Sure, Biden reminded us, he had worked for Barack Obama, a president who had voiced outright contempt for the fossil fuel industry in the past. Sure, he had said a few things about wanting to embrace green energy to protect our environment, and he had often referred to climate change as an "existential threat."

But back then, he promised to come up with a "middle ground" on climate policy—one that would appeal to people who were concerned about the environment *and* blue-collar voters who worked on pipelines and oil rigs. One of his top aides said that while he "respected" the far-left activist groups who dominated the debate at the time, his candidate had "learned from the Obama administration" that "unless [they] find middle ground on these issues, [they] risk not having any policies."[13]

At the time, more than half of the Democratic Party's clown car candidates had backed Alexandria Ocasio-Cortez's Green New Deal. Now in case you've forgotten, the Green New Deal was a hilarious list of liberal demands concerning the environment (with all sorts of money going to unrelated liberal causes thrown in as well). Its main pitch was phasing out all carbon-emitting power plants fueled by coal and oil by 2030, with their replacement by power plants fueled by wind and solar. They had also vowed to ban any further drilling by oil companies on federal lands, a practice which had yielded hundreds of thousands of gallons of oil, much of which the United States was able to export to other countries. The final price tag of the whole thing was estimated to be somewhere around $93 trillion, which I think you'll agree is a lot even today, *after* two years of Biden inflation.

But Joe Biden, we were promised, would not agree to the nutty Green New Deal agenda. He wanted to be a president for all Americans. The takedown of our oil industry wasn't even on Biden's mind. (Granted, *nothing* was on Biden's mind, other than Corn Pop monologues or wondering where his next Ben & Jerry's ice cream cone would come from.)

But at some point, Biden turned into one of them.

The seeds of Biden going green was possibly May of 2019, when AOC appeared onstage at an event that was meant to drum up support for her Green New Deal that had been unveiled three months earlier. Rather than hyping her pipe dream of a bill that night, however, AOC spent most of her stage time taking subtle shots at Biden, a candidate she had already gone on record as saying did not "particularly animate" her.

"I will be damned," she said, "if the same politicians who refused to act then are going to try to come back today and say, 'We need a middle-of-the-road approach to save our lives.'"[14]

The political press was full of stories the next day about how Biden wasn't proposing radical enough solutions to important, life-or-death issues. Several predicted he wouldn't make it more than a few months into the primaries. In response, Team Biden strapped on their Birkenstocks, put on their aviators, and came up with an *extra* radical climate plan. One that they rushed out a few weeks later. It was called "The Biden Plan for a Clean Energy Revolution and Environmental Justice," and it promised to go "beyond the Obama-Biden Administration platform on climate."

Now, not only was Biden going to shut down fossil fuel companies; he was going to "stand up to the abuse of power by polluters who disproportionately harm communities of color." While "everyone is already feeling the effects of climate change," according to the plan, "the impacts . . . are far more acute on communities of color, tribal lands, and low-income communities."[15]

Really? You're telling me that to the already extremely long list of things that are racist in the eyes of the Radical Left—the justice system, college admissions, mathematics, the nuclear family, baseball, apple pie, the words "Master Bedroom"—we are now adding *the sun*? Honestly, if I mapped out even one-tenth of the things the modern Left calls racist, it would take up not just the rest of this book but several additional volumes. And of course, all that paper to print the books would involve cutting down an entire forest. As a concession to the Left, I'll refrain from doing this—*for the sake of the environment*.

Now, if you're wondering how the Biden team came up with so many far-left positions so quickly, you might take a closer look at the actual content of this plan. When a reporter from the *Daily Wire* did just that a few hours after it was released, he found that not everything in the document came straight from Joe's head. (Surprise, surprise.) Instead, it turns out that most of the actual language was lifted—and, in at least five cases, directly plagiarized—from some of the most popular far-left climate groups in the country. In other words, Biden (or rather, puppeteer of the moment) heard AOC's mild criticism about how non-radical he was, freaked out, and then did a sloppy cut-and-paste job on all the most radical climate plans he could find, and then put his name at the top of the paper.

Anyone familiar with the first time Joe Biden ran for president, back in 1988, will not be surprised by this. During that race, he plagiarized a whole speech from Neil Kinnock, the then-leader of Britain's left-wing Labour Party. That time, Biden stole the chap's whole life story and attributed it to himself.[16]

When that bit of plagiarism came to light, Biden at least had the decency to drop out of the race. This time, his team updated a few footnotes, issued a quick apology, and got on with the campaign. The Left will overlook all manner of personal sins (and obvious signs of cognitive decline) if it means they can continue to victimize America and gain power.

Thanks to his desperation to win the presidency, Biden adopted every aspect of the Radical Left's anti-fossil fuel Green New Deal agenda. And he did so in a way that was shameless, dishonest, and hypocritical, even by the all-time sleazy standard Joe has set for these sorts of things. His father was a car salesman, but even he would have been impressed by Joe's standards for hoodwinking.

Today, whenever he's asked about climate change or fossil fuels, Biden gets up like the Manchurian Candidate and recites his lines. During a campaign stop in June of 2022, for instance, a little girl on the side of the stage said the code words—"climate change"—and the performance began. Biden looked around, ambled over to the girl, and leaned in *very* close—close enough to find out what brand of shampoo she uses—to say:

"Kiddo, I want you to just take a look," he said. "I want you to look in my eyes. I guarantee—I *guarantee* that we are going to end fossil fuels and I am not going to cooperate."[17]

In true Communist fashion, the radicals took this old man and sent him to a reeducation camp. Now, he's back, and fully on board with the revolution.

Whether he was a true believer or simply thoroughly reeducated, from the moment he set foot in the Oval Office, this one-man wannabe wrecking ball displayed an open hostility toward our entire energy sector. On his first day, he canceled construction of the Keystone XL pipeline, a 1,179-mile-long structure that would have piped oil from Canada to the Gulf of Mexico, thereby further reducing our dependence on foreign oil. As soon as Biden signed that order, an estimated 11,000 jobs—architects, construction workers, and rig workers—went up in smoke. Just minutes later, in another of his day-one orders, Biden canceled new oil drilling leases in Alaska, citing a "lack of industry interest."[18]

Criminal lies.

Climate activists, in between traveling by private jet to their latest climate conference, cheered each and every one of these moves. John Kerry, possibly the only man in America who looks more corpse-like than Joe Biden, touted the move overseas, traveling around (by jet) for his newly-invented job of U.S. Special Presidential Envoy for Climate.

The hits kept coming. Shortly after his Day-One executive order spree, Biden halted new drilling leases in Alaska's Arctic National

Wildlife Refuge (ANWR). A week later, he banned new oil and gas leases on federal lands and waters, and in June of 2021 he shut down exploration on existing leases in ANWR. In October, he increased the regulatory burdens on building pipelines and other infrastructure. In February 2022, he limited leasing in Alaska's National Petroleum Reserve.

Strange. For a man who's got a long list of unkept promises from the campaign—to "shut down the virus," for instance, or to "unify the country"—he's really sticking to this whole "stop the oil companies from drilling" thing.

Why?

The answer is simple, and it's got very little to do with Biden (a man who couldn't care less about fossil fuel companies).

The culprits, as usual, are the ideologues educated in our own school system (and up until the pandemic hidden from parents) who have now taken over the White House. These are radical young aides, and they believe that climate change is an existential threat to our planet. Recent studies have shown that record numbers of people from their generation truly believe that they will be killed as a result of climate change. About 57 percent of these panic-attack Millennials have experienced "climate-induced anxiety" caused by the stress of knowing our world will soon "burn up and become uninhabitable."[19]

Democrats cater to no one other than their own neurotic, climate-obsessed base. Everyone else—especially ordinary middle-class Americans who need to drive cars, cook food, and heat their homes in the winter—does not matter.

In their eyes, we're in the middle of a revolution. High gas prices are just the sacrifice we'll have to make to transition from a prosperous, energy-independent country into one that reduces its carbon footprint by a few percentage points every year. This is the same justification that has been used for centuries by rulers who wanted to radically transform their societies. During the Great Leap Forward of the mid-twentieth century, Chairman Mao assured Chinese farmers who suddenly had to send their harvests to a central authority that it was a small price to pay for a complete overhaul of the country's agricultural system. Stalin did the same thing when he came to power in the Soviet Union.

Both men, of course, were lying. They knew that their bright ideas weren't going to work, which is why they had to *force* people to go along with them in the first place. The Radical Left of today is no different. They offer you the freedom of doing and saying exactly what they want—before they force you to do it.

During a press conference in Japan, when asked about the high gas prices that were crippling American citizens, Biden brushed it all aside. He was all but winking to the Green Energy Goblins feeding him his lines from the wings.

"[When] it comes to the gas prices," he said, "we're going through an incredible transition that is taking place that, God willing, when it's over, we'll be stronger, and the world will be stronger and less reliant on fossil fuels when this is over."[20] Biden was actually praising high gas prices, but insisting that he is obsessed with lowering gas prices. Not enough, however, to unleash American energy independence.

Brian Deese, Director of the National Economic Council, was asked about President Biden's comments blaming Russia for rising gas prices. In answer to the question "What do you say to families that can't afford to pay $4.85 a gallon?" Deese responded, "What you heard from the President today was a clear articulation of the stakes. This is about the future of the *liberal world order* and we have to stand firm." The globalists seeking to take down America are willing to let you know that it is a new liberal world order that they are seeking. They are so confident of their success at taking down America that they no longer try to gaslight us. They believe that under Biden they have accomplished their goal, and they aren't afraid to admit it.

This environmentalist insanity was brought to us by a moody Swedish teenager, power-crazed politicians like Gavin Newsom, and the unstable aides and ideologues surrounding Joe Biden. They not only hate fossil fuels, but they hate everything those fuels have done to improve the lives of everyday Americans and create the super-power that America is today. Fossil fuels are what powers us, literally. So as part of the takedown, those fossil fuels have to go.

The Misinformation Game

The takedown of any nation or culture, especially from within, starts with division. If it is not to be a violent revolution, but instead a more silent, creeping one, speech would be a convenient place to start. There have always been objective truths where there can be little disagreement. The fight begins in the gray areas where opinions most often differ. It is these areas the Left has been expert at co-opting and controlling. These decisions instead are based on their narrative, not the truths developed in the time-honored tradition of cross examination as in a courtroom. They do it by sheer force of peer pressure, social media, and with the consequence of cancellation.

But you may ask, isn't the First Amendment and free speech one of the fundamental pillars of our Republic? The right to say what we think without being censored by the government or anyone else for that matter. The sad truth is that the battle for free speech in the last decade in this country has been won by the Left, beginning with political correctness, their opinion of what is hate speech, and the literal shutdown of other speech. It was shocking how freedom of speech, so fundamental to a free society—even for the Left—was totally controlled by their narrative.

It first hit me on September 25 of 2012 when then-President Barack Obama spoke at the United Nations with that green marble wall behind him as he said, "the future most not belong to those who slander the prophet of Islam."[1] I remember thinking to myself: *Slandering the prophet of Islam? Haven't we just had First Amendment discussions about the right to put the crucifix of Jesus in urine and call it "Piss Christ"? And the funding of a painting called "Mary in the Dung" with the Virgin Mary surrounded by manure?* The free-speech proponents argued that these tax-funded exhibits on display, no matter how distasteful, were protected by the First Amendment. Yet here the president of the United States was taking a position that there should be no future for those who slander the prophet (Muhammad) of Islam.

It was at that point the battle for free speech accelerated. Fail to toe the liberal line on any important issue (and plenty of unimportant ones), and the media and the Democrats will label you a purveyor of "misinformation." Whether the issue now is Covid, Ukraine, Hunter's laptop, or the 2020 election results, as far as they're concerned "The data is in," "The experts have spoken," or their very favorite, "The science is settled." Sometimes, the science has settled more than once, in contradictory ways. This is all part of a well-established strategy.

The Left starts their attack on free speech beginning on our leftist college campuses, which serve as a kind of scientific laboratory for their radical agenda, and then over the years they start moving beyond the campus and implementing their repressive speech code policies and social taboos throughout other institutions. Wait a second. A dangerous virus grown in a lab and eventually spreading throughout the rest of the world and wrecking civilization? Please, stop me if you've heard this one before.

Before the Left started labeling everything as "misinformation," the go-to phrase was "hate speech." On campuses during the first wave of political correctness college students who tried to defend America or Israel were apt to be condemned for spreading "hate speech." The Left would typically say they were all for *free* speech, but not "hate speech" which evidently was something quite different. I suspect they would be surprised to learn that the United States Supreme Court vehemently differs from their asinine interpretation of hate speech. In the landmark case of *Brandenburg v. Ohio* "a state may not forbid even advocating the use of force or unlawful conduct unless the advocacy is directed to inciting or producing imminent lawless action."[2] The hate speech involved in this KKK case as abominable as it was, was protected by the First Amendment.

Today they transitioned from hate speech to misinformation. They're all for free speech, but not for "misinformation." And who gets to decide what is hate speech or misinformation? They do, of course.

The brilliance of the "misinformation" rhetoric is that it muzzles the Left's foes where the hate speech charges do not. Sure, if you're debating Black Lives Matter or immigration or transgenderism, smearing your opponent's arguments as "hate speech" is easy. But what if the debate is about Hunter Biden's corruption, or the outcome of an election, or the best way to handle a pandemic? Calling the debate surrounding those issues "hate speech" is a challenge (not that they haven't tried!). "Misinformation" silences your opponent while seeming to sidestep the issue of free speech. Instead of a person being censored for being hateful, you just censor them for "misinformation." How simple!

But that's not to say the Left is pulling its rhetorical punch. Not at all. "Misinformation" might sound like a kinder label than "hate speech," but not in the Left's hands. Because in the Left's moral universe, sharing unapproved facts isn't a mark of independence or a sign of being misguided or even a display of gullibility. It's the first step on the road to *fascism*.

In 2021, members of the Biden administration stated that anyone with concerns about the way the 2020 election was conducted was not only spreading misinformation, but was also displaying fascist tendencies. This was especially rich, considering that you have to go back to George H. W. Bush's victory in 1988 to find the last presidential election that Democrats admit Republicans won fair and square (Dukakis losing California as a Democrat helps).

Even those who accepted Joe Biden's win in 2020 but have a few lingering concerns about, say, mail-in ballots and the potential for fraud, are called fascists who shouldn't be welcome in polite (or even impolite) society. That countries such as France have made mail-in ballots illegal for fear of fraud is something liberals have put out of their minds—or rather, never allowed into it in the first place.

In May of 2021, Jake Tapper said that anyone who supported the "Big Lie" of election denial would not be invited on his CNN show, *State of the Union*. In drawing this line in the sand, Tapper insisted that he was keeping the world safe from "Election Liars," making sure to note what a threat to democracy these people posed.

Let's hold him to his new rule. In that case he should consider canceling White House Press Secretary Karine Jean-Pierre, who has been a regular on his show. In December 2016, less than a month after the election of President Trump, Karine Jean-Pierre tweeted, "Stolen emails, stolen drone, stolen election . . . welcome to the world of #unpresidented Trump."[3] From 2016 until Trump's last day in office, Jean-Pierre and the rest of the supposedly principled Democrats continued to push the lie that it was Vladimir Putin and a shady group of Russian hackers, not millions of Americans, who put Donald Trump in the White House. Every time they did so, they implicitly—and sometimes *explicitly*, in the case of Karine Jean-Pierre—said that the 2016 election had been illegitimate, and that our democracy was now firmly under the control of a foreign power.

A History of Denial

Of course, KJP is by no means the biggest Democrat to engage in election denial. In 2001, former president Bill Clinton thought Al Gore should have been the winner of the 2000 presidential election, "and the only way [the Republicans] could win the election was to *stop* the voting in Florida,"[4] with Debbie Wasserman Schultz adding (D-FL) in 2016 that Al Gore "won Florida."[5] In 2008, then-Sen. Barack Obama made a joke about Bush stealing the 2004 election, saying it helps that in Ohio "Democrats are in charge of the [voting] machines."[6] Former President Jimmy Carter had also remarked that, "Trump didn't actually win the election in 2016; he lost the election, and he was put into office because the Russians interfered."[7] Back in 2000, Carter said he believed "Al Gore was elected president" rather than George W. Bush.[8] Had Carter not lost to Ronald Reagan by 10 points and 440 electoral votes in one of the worst landslides ever, I'm sure he'd still be blaming his own loss on Iranian sheikhs. Representative Maxine "Get in Their Faces" Waters of California has cast doubt on every presidential election that produced a Republican win since 2000. Let's not forget that Imperious Hillary Clinton has told everyone who would listen that her election was "stolen from her." Please, next time Hillary is blaming someone for stealing the 2016 election from her, make sure there's a mirror in the room and that she's facing it.

When it comes to charges of "misinformation" in regards to election-denying, the Democrats have a standard. The double standard.

Georgia on Their Mind

Stacey Abrams was one of the biggest Democrat celebrities of 2018. Her campaign raised tens of millions of dollars from around the country, based on the promise she would turn Georgia's state government blue. Unfortunately for Democrats, it didn't happen. So Democrats doubled down—with their own brand of misinformation. Americans were told that Georgia, once part of the Confederate South, was again engaging in the ugliest form of discrimination—that black voters were being suppressed. Because of this racial hatred, Democrats said, Stacey Abrams lost to Brian Kemp.

Democrats would seethe further when Brian Kemp signed into law a bill that included new restrictions on voting by mail, and greater legislative control over how elections are run. With the Democrats taking L's on Stacey Abrams and then on Georgia's new voting laws, they sought out someone to punish. I'm afraid there are no prizes for guessing the Left chose average Americans to be their victims.

Small business owners in Atlanta who wanted to see the Major League Baseball All-Star Game that summer were punished for passing the voter fraud bill when the league (under immense pressure from activists) moved the venue to Denver. These businesses, and their employees, were punished because corporate America bought the Abrams-Biden lie that Georgia's voting law was the return of Jim Crow.

But you know what they say about karma and the things that go around coming around. Stacey Abrams can tell you. In 2022, with another chance to prove how loved she was in Georgia, Abrams fell flat on her face in her bid for the governorship—again. That race saw a record number of Georgians cast their ballot. Brian Kemp beat her again, and beat her handily. So much for voter suppression.

After Abrams's first loss to Kemp, Jean-Pierre tweeted, "Yes—the race was stolen." The next year, she tweeted the message, "Reminder: Brian Kemp stole the gubernatorial election from Georgians and Stacey Abrams."[9]

When a Republican asserts that it is *possible* mail-in ballots and lack of voter ID might allow for a stolen election, they are preaching fascism and not welcome on CNN (not that they should be going on anyway). Corporate America is mustered to boycott them. When a liberal accuses conservatives of "stealing" an election, they are simply grabbing one rung of the ladder that will carry them all the way to the job of White House Press Secretary, followed by a cushy cable news pundit gig.

The slandering of Georgia by Democrats was a textbook case of misinformation, and they paid no price.

Pointing the Finger

The double standard with liberals and the media is always there, almost regardless of the issue. A Democrat's unsubstantiated whining is considered to be a valid argument, whereas a Republican's identical claim, no matter how much evidence they muster, can be dismissed as "misinformation." An undeniable blunder from a Democrat is a wholesome mistake, while a Republican's error is presumed to be in bad faith. Republicans are always sneaking fascism into America, while Democrats *could never.*

In reality, nothing could be further from the truth.

On August 25, 2022, Biden delivered a speech to a gathering of Maryland Democrats in which he added a new term to his rhetorical arsenal.

"The MAGA Republicans don't just threaten our personal rights and economic security," Biden said. "They're a threat to our very democracy. They refuse to accept the will of the people. They embrace—embrace—political violence." Biden then said the problem with the GOP was "not just Trump, it's the entire philosophy that underpins the—I'm going to say something—it's like *semi-fascism.*"[10]

Just a few days after maligning half the voting public as adherents of one of the most loathsome ideologies in history, Biden traveled to Philadelphia to give another speech in front of Independence Hall, the historic building where our Declaration of Independence was signed and our Constitution drafted. While Rockin' Chair Joe has spent more than a quarter of his presidency at his Delaware vacation home, apparently he can occasionally be moved to ditch the swimming trunks, put down the ice cream cone, and deliver a rambling semi-coherent address to a large crowd.

The results get more disturbing with every speech.

In the days leading up to this address, several commentators predicted that Biden would tone down his message. Surely, they said, not even Divider-in-Chief Joe Biden would stand in front of such a potent symbol of America to label his political opponents as enemies of the state. They predicted "the great unifier" would give a speech on the soul of the nation. Even the *New York Post* editorial board, which does not usually give Biden the benefit of the doubt, predicted he "probably won't roll out the 'semi-fascist' charge in his Thursday night speech (unless he goes off-script)."[11]

The *Post* gets so much right that we'll have to forgive them for getting this so wrong.

Around seven o'clock in the evening, Biden arrived in Philadelphia, surrounded by a Secret Service cocoon that protected him from the city's record-setting homicide rate. He ascended to a podium flanked by blood-red lights, which gave the impression that Biden was speaking from the lair of a comic book villain instead of the City of Brotherly Love. Behind him stood two solemn rifle-toting Marines in white gloves. Had George W. Bush or Donald Trump given a speech like this in such an ominous setting, liberals would've gone into seizure.

From the time Joe Biden took the stage, it was clear that our cool, aviator-sporting, "C'mon, man"-in-Chief would not be making an appearance that evening. Instead, we saw a creepy grandpa dictator who seemed intent on stirring up as much division as possible. Toward the middle of his address, Biden turned once again to the millions of people who'd voted against him in the 2020 election.

"MAGA forces," he said, "are determined to take this country backwards—backwards to an America where there is no right to choose, no right to privacy, no right to contraception, no right to marry who you love. They promote authoritarian leaders, and they fanned the flames of political violence that are a threat to our personal rights, to the pursuit of justice, to the rule of law, to the very soul of this country."[12]

Biden dragged in MAGA every chance he could, trying to gin up the energy he needed to unite Democrats. He was uniting them against Donald Trump, a man who wasn't even running!

Joe accused his political opponents of doing something that he was clearly guilty of himself. It was not MAGA Republicans who were attempting to stoke "fear, division, and darkness," but the Democrats, who seemed to realize that the only way they could avoid getting clobbered in a red wave midterm election was to terrify and *misinform* low-information members of the public into thinking that the other side presented a grave "threat to democracy."

In Michigan, a moderate Republican representative, Peter Meijer, was running for reelection. On paper, Representative Meijer agreed with almost everything the Democrats stood for. He was one of few Republicans to vote to impeach President Trump after he left office, and he did not deny the Biden election results. But instead of simply running their candidate against moderate Meijer, the Democratic Committee for Campaign Contributions decided to run ads to boost his primary opponent—someone who *did* deny the results of the 2020 election, which is what they've been warning us against for years. This kind of rhetoric to them was not a "threat to democracy" or "creeping fascism." After all, their end would justify any means.

Like a bunch of Jussie Smolletts, the Democrats needed to create fake threats. To use another word for it, they needed . . . *misinformation.* In 2022, the Democrats' goal was to paint MAGA Republicans as extremists and portray themselves as moderate defenders of democracy. Therefore, it was in the best interest of Democrats to run MAGA Republican candidates in moderate districts. The Democrats *like* when they can accuse people of being threats to democracy.

Of course, whether actively putting money into the primary campaigns of the people you would prefer to face in the general election is itself a kind of "election interference" is something I leave up to you to decide.

Sticks and Stones

They've called us names, insulted our beliefs, and called for us to be removed from polite society. Thanks to their almost complete infiltration of the media, they have done this with impunity.

I'm not talking about politicians attacking one another on the campaign trail. That is perfectly normal. That kind of thing has been happening since before the country was founded. During the first major presidential election the country ever had, in fact, Founding Fathers Thomas Jefferson and John Adams hurled horrible insults at one another. In one pamphlet, Jefferson referred to Adams as a "hermaphrodite." In response, Adams said that electing Jefferson would lead to "prostitution, incest, and adultery" becoming common in the White House.[13] (For those tactics, Democrats today would call Jefferson a "transphobe" and accuse Adams of "slut-shaming" those engaged in "sex work." Better rip some more statues down!)

The rhetoric back then was somehow even worse in the House and the Senate. Throughout the 1800s, as tensions began rising between North and South, congressional deliberations often devolved into name-calling and outright violence. In those days, when Democrats—and it was *always* Democrats—rose to defend the institution of slavery, it wasn't uncommon for them to punctuate their remarks with violent outbursts. During one debate in 1856, South Carolina Congressman Preston Brooks nearly killed Senator Charles Sumner of Massachusetts when he savagely beat him with a cane for giving a powerful anti-slavery speech.[14]

Nevertheless, as American democracy moved into the twentieth century, certain rules developed to govern partisan attacks. Families were usually off-limits. So were accusations that a rival was unpatriotic or engaged in lewd personal activities.

But most importantly, candidates did not attack voters. They did not say, or even insinuate, that entire portions of the American electorate were not worth speaking to.

As you know, that is no longer the case.

The mainstream media networks were silent in 2008, for instance, when then-Senator Barack Obama, at an expensive fundraiser no less, said it "wasn't surprising" that Americans who had lost their jobs thanks to the globalist policies of President Bill Clinton were "bitter." The media didn't care when Obama said that these people "cling to guns or religion or antipathy toward people who aren't like them or anti-immigrant sentiment or anti-trade sentiment as a way to explain their frustrations."[15]

The reason the media didn't care about those remarks is painfully simple: they agreed with them. They just couldn't say so themselves on the air yet. But a few years later, when Obama became president, that was no longer the case. During his administration, it was common to have CNN anchors talk about people in middle America as if they were conquering imperialists talking about the ignorant natives. They came to believe that anyone not fortunate enough to have been born in some wealthy enclave on either coast was somehow stupid, bigoted, and not even worth listening to.

It's no wonder that when it came time to decide which of the leading Democrats would succeed Obama in the White House, the entire mainstream media threw its support behind the most smug, superior creature ever to emerge from the Deep State Swamp.

It was almost exactly eight years after Obama made his first crack about guns and religion that Crooked Hillary Clinton—the person Obama had personally chosen to succeed him as president, believing even then that Joe was too old for the job—got up at another glitzy

East Coast fundraiser to rile up the Democrat base. I'm sure that activists in the audience were not disappointed.

At the podium, Hillary Clinton, with all the subtlety of a street preacher, informed the audience: "I am all that stands between you and the apocalypse." For the next few minutes, it was your typical accusations—that her opponent was racist, sexist, etc.

But then came that special twist that sent Hillary's speech viral.

"Just to be grossly generalistic," she said, "you could put half of Trump's supporters in what I call the basket of deplorables. Right? The racist, sexist, homophobic, xenophobic, Islamophobic—you name it. And unfortunately, there are people like that. And he has lifted them up."[16]

There it is, folks. *That* is the perfect blend of entitlement, narcissism, and downright cruelty that is necessary for anyone who wants to join the ranks of the liberal elite. And until Biden gave his creepy, unhinged rant about fascists in Philadelphia, no one had ever nailed that combination quite as well as Hillary Clinton. When you look at the words she spoke—and the demeaning, superior manner in which she spoke them—you can see traces of everything that would come later: the weaponization of the government against school board parents, the widespread bans from social media, the insistence that ordinary Americans are "fascists" because they dared to support one candidate over another in the election of 2020. In speaking the way she did—carrying the rhetoric of Barack Obama one step further—Hillary Clinton made it possible for an entire segment of the American electorate to be written off as racist, evil, and unworthy of membership in polite society.

In so much of politics, the first step is sadly to unite the people against a common enemy. The best way to do this, as any schoolyard bully knows, is through ridicule and name-calling. The Democrats know that when you attack real people—the kind who have families, jobs, and real concerns about the direction of their communities— you'll soon expose yourself for the bully that you are. (The media dragged high school Trump supporter Nick Sandmann's name through the mud, but his later financial settlement from NBC for slandering him is exhibit A that this treatment from the media can backfire on them.[17])

Liberals have learned, however, that when you attack "MAGA Republicans" or "fascists" *as a group*, you'll have a much easier time convincing the masses that these people are, in fact, the enemies of democracy and decency. You must first dehumanize a group before you can slander and even advocate violence against them. For example, back in 2017, do you remember the Left saying it was good to punch "Nazis"?[18] The strategy behind that "punch a Nazi" rhetoric was that if it's wrong to punch people but *morally acceptable to punch a "Nazi,"* then you'll soon find the definition of a Nazi has been expanded to include almost all of your political enemies. And sure enough, soon people who were anything but radical right-wingers were being accosted by left-wing mobs. By misinforming the nation and painting about a third of the American electorate as far-right extremists, the Democrats subtly justified violence and bullying against Republicans.

It should come as no surprise, then, that Biden and the Democrats have begun to use these terms and tactics to refer not only to people who openly support Donald Trump, but to anyone who votes Republican for any reason. Biden is lying through his fake teeth when he says he's not using this term to refer to "all Republicans," as he did during his campaign blitz last summer. In fact, just a few lines later in the same speech, he lumps "election deniers" in with people who support conservative policies such as abortion bans and opposition to same-sex marriage. (According to this standard, by the way, every faithful member of the Catholic Church—a group that *supposedly* includes Biden himself—is a "MAGA Republican" who threatens democracy.) A few days later, during a Labor Day address, Biden again said the "extreme MAGA Republicans" were "full of anger, violence, hate, and division."[19]

Of course, he didn't come up with these words all on his own. Instead, he tapped the well-known historian and political commentator Jon Meacham, a professor at Vanderbilt University who once claimed on MSNBC that Republicans used only their "lizard brains" when deciding which candidates to support. In the lead-up to the 2020 election, Meacham gave a quiz in one of the courses he was teaching that included this question: "Was the Constitution designed to perpetuate white supremacy and protect the institution of slavery?" Any student who responded "no"—the objectively correct answer from a historical standpoint—got the question wrong. Whether he's writing a quiz or writing a speech, Jon Meacham is propagating *misinformation*.

It's not only the professors and elected officials, either. Most often, these attacks come from political pundits, Hollywood actors, and members of the financial elite who live in liberal echo chambers where they never have to hear anything that makes them even slightly uncomfortable. To them, everyone who votes Republican—everyone who doesn't live in their particular section of Los Angeles or Manhattan, in fact—is stupid, racist, and, as of a few months ago, a new "threat to democracy."

Of course, it's not only overpaid former political consultants who talk down to the rest of the country and make their careers on bullying people like a bunch of children. It's the aforementioned

Hollywood actors too. In June of 2022, the comedian Wanda Sykes appeared on the *Late Show* with Stephen Colbert. A few days before her appearance, the Supreme Court had released its landmark decision in *Dobbs*, which returned the decision about whether to outlaw abortion to state governments.

What did the astute political commentator Wanda Sykes have to say about it?

"It just sucks, man," she said. "It really does, you know? It's like the country, it is no longer a democracy, right. We're—it's no longer majority rules." A few seconds later, she said that to her, the problem was "that middle stuff. It is those states in the middle. The red stuff. Why do they get to tell us what to do when the majority of us live out in New York, California, and we are paying for all this crap. Really. I mean, right? We're footing the bill."[20]

There are so many idiocies in that statement that it's hard to know where to begin, but I'll try.

First of all, those "middle" people are, presumably, the ones who tune in and watch whatever awful sitcoms you're on, so I would be a little nicer to them if I were you. You're insulting your own audience. As for this business about New York and California "footing the bill" for everyone else, you might want to check the labels on your food the next time your assistant comes back from the grocery store. I would bet all the money in Wanda's bank account that most of it was grown and produced in those "middle states" she seems to hate so much.

When did people begin to believe it was acceptable to speak about their fellow citizens this way? This is something that genuinely baffles me. These liberals have labeled any facts that contradict their insane beliefs "misinformation," and they have attempted to silence

us by using vague threats of cancellation to intimidate us into submission. It's no surprise that they've moved from ideas to people,
labeling anyone who dares to be a conservative in the year 2022 a
"semi-fascist," to use Biden's term.

When it comes to Joe Biden, the warning signs have been here
for quite a while. In March of 2021, while he was attempting to
justify locking millions of American citizens in their homes to avoid
further infections from Covid—a disease that we had all realized was
not nearly as dangerous as we feared—Biden turned his ire on the
Republican governors who were lifting mask mandates and allowing
their citizens to go outside again. For most of us, this represented
real progress in the fight against power-hungry liberals and the so-
called experts who wanted to keep us locked down forever. To Biden,
however, these governors were dumb cavemen.

"The last thing we need," he said, "is this Neanderthal thinking
that in the meantime everything's fine, take off your mask, forget it."[21]

When he realized he could get away with that, he started ratchet-
ing up the language, as all wannabee authoritarians have done since
time immemorial. After "Neanderthals," we got "semi-fascist," then
just "fascist."

For years, the Radical Left and their allies in the corporate press
have been shutting down the free speech of ordinary Americans. You
might think that the only reason they've done this is pure sport—
just trying to cancel as many people as possible to make themselves
feel better. But anyone who does not take them seriously is under-
estimating the extent to which the Radical Left has been planning
to take us down from the beginning. The Left is waging a war
on American freedoms every day. Every day that goes by, another
indoctrinated student of the Left graduates to work in America's

business and government to promote their agenda. Every day that goes by, more and more Americans become accustomed to being censored and having their speech shut down. Every day that goes by, the pillars of America crumble. I'm sure they'd love to flag that as "misinformation."

CLOSING STATEMENT

Rome, and America, weren't built in a day. But while Rome also took a long time to fall, America is on the point of being lost in a single generation.

Assuming there are still historians in the future, I like to think they will be fascinated by the decline and destruction of America. They will look at this country during this time we are living in now and wonder *How did she hit rock bottom so quickly? How did this country choose leaders like Biden, Obama, and the Clintons who are draining the life out of our once-exceptional nation through socialist and anti-capitalist policies?* A dead America will make quite the autopsy.

In just a few short decades, the Radical Left took America from absolute superpower to a state in crisis. And in barely two years, the Biden Left has undone the recovery of President Trump and then some. We aren't worrying about whether America will be great in fifty years. Now, we're worrying about whether America will be *intact* in ten years.

The Left is in the process of turning America into an unexceptional nation. It's not that corrupt or senile leaders like Joe Biden are unheard of. They've appeared plenty of times in countries you can read about in the "World" section of a news website. But they've never been the norm *in America*. Not in the unstoppable superpower I grew up in. In the America I grew up in, you had the right to expect better from your country. Can we still say that today?

I still believe this country can be turned around. But what would have been easy to fix ten or twenty or fifty years ago will be difficult to fix now. Sometimes I think it will take nothing short of a spiritual revival, not unlike the ones seen in previous centuries of American history, to bring us back from the moral abyss we are currently on the precipice of.

But call me an optimist. I still think there is a way to rebuild America. There is a way to give Americans faith that everyone is equal under the law, but it will take hard work and leaders who aren't afraid. Leaders who can no longer game the system. Getting better leaders starts with demanding them. We can't treat the disasters of Joe and Hunter Biden as acceptable. We need to know we have the right to expect better. We need to have guts.

Above all, we need to recognize that what has happened to America isn't an accident or a mistake. It was a crime by those who resented the shining city on the hill that Ronald Reagan so eloquently spoke of.

Election 2024 is right around the corner. We don't have much time. The first question you should ask of any candidate is whether they love this country and whether they believe in the Constitution. And not just at the presidential level. If we have learned anything these past few years, it is that for all the power of the federal government, our statehouses, local governments, district attorneys, sheriffs, and school boards wield enormous power over our lives and our futures. They are the ones who decide whether laws are enforced or ignored. They are the ones who decide whether schools teach reading or race hatred. Find the people who are committing these atrocities against

America and toss them out of office. And then—this is the important part—*never let them back in.* These crimes against America must be punished with a lifelong exile from the halls of power.

By noticing the crimes against America and having the courage to put an end to them we can restore this nation as the world's one truly exceptional country. We will again be a place that no longer tolerates the kind of petty tyrants, woke gangsters, foreign looters, and criminal crack addict First Sons described in these pages. My hope is that 2024 will mark the start of a national awakening, and decades from now my grandchildren will be able to describe the America they grew up in as still being the greatest country on earth.

ACKNOWLEDGMENTS

I am grateful to my entire family—I love you all. Thank you for the continued support, patience, and laughter.

Thank you to all my readers, viewers, and listeners. It is a privilege to be able to join you in your homes every evening on television, radio, and through my many books. Each one of you is a Patriot. Never give up.

Deep appreciation to Winning Team Publishing, especially Sergio Gor, Donald Trump Jr., Connor Hickey, Amanda Varian, and everyone else involved in making this tome a success.

I am grateful to the entire Fox News Channel family, especially my co-hosts on *The Five*.

Thank you to my Poodles—Ted, Red, and Stella—who are always happy to sit quietly as I write.

Finally, I am beyond thankful to live on the greatest nation on earth, the United States of America—I just hope we will be able to pass American exceptionalism, opportunity, and security to our grandchildren.

NOTES

Count One: A Breach of Sovereignty

[1] Julia Ainsley, "Migrant border crossings in fiscal year 2022 topped 2.76 million, breaking previous record," NBC News, October 22, 2022, https://www.nbcnews.com/politics/immigration/migrant-border -crossings-fiscal-year-2022-topped-276-million-breaking-rcna53517.

[2] Miriam Jordan, "Smuggling Migrants at the Border Now a Billion-Dollar Business," *New York Times*, July 25, 2022, https://www.ny times.com/2022/07/25/us/migrant-smuggling-evolution.html.

[3] Christopher Cadelago and Olivia Olander, "Biden calls Trump's philosophy 'semi-fascism,'" *Politico*, August 25, 2022, https:// www.politico.com/news/2022/08/25/biden-trump-philosophy -semi-fascism-00053831.

[4] Yasmeen Abutaleb and Marisa Iati, "Biden warns U.S. faces powerful threat from anti-democratic forces," *Washington Post*, September 1, 2022, https://www.washingtonpost.com/politics/2022/09/01/biden -slams-attacks-on-democracy/.

Count Two: Perjury

[1] Michael Goodwin, "FBI, Big Tech, Big Media: Partners in collusion," *New York Post*, December 3, 2022, https://nypost.com/2022/12/03/fbi-big-tech-big-media-partners-in-collusion/.

[2] Bradford Betz, "Joe Biden botches Declaration of Independence quote during Texas rally," Fox 32 Chicago, March 3, 2020, https://www.fox32chicago.com/news/joe-biden-botches-declaration-of-independence-quote-during-texas-rally.

[3] Harriet Alexander, Katelyn Caralle, and Josh Porter, "Hunter Biden associate referred to 'the big guy' in SECOND message during panic about laptop leaks," *Daily Mail*, July 28, 2022, https://www.dailymail.co.uk/news/article-11056505/Hunter-Biden-associate-referred-Big-Guy-SECOND-message.html.

[4] Lois Beckett, "At least 25 Americans were killed during protest and political unrest in 2020," *The Guardian*, October 31, 2020, https://www.theguardian.com/world/2020/oct/31/americans-killed-protests-political-unrest-acled.

[5] Aamer Madhani, "Biden: I never talked to son Hunter about overseas business dealings," *USA Today*, September 21, 2019, https://www.usatoday.com/story/news/politics/elections/2019/09/21/joe-biden-never-talked-ukraine-son-trump-needs-investigated/2401830001/.

[6] Emma-Jo Morris and Gabrielle Fonrouge, "Smoking-gun email reveals how Hunter Biden introduced Ukrainian businessman to VP dad," *New York Post*, October 14, 2020, https://nypost.com/2020/10/14/email-reveals-how-hunter-biden-introduced-ukrainian-biz-man-to-dad/.

[7] Morris and Fonrouge, "Smoking-gun emails."

8 "Public Statement on the Hunter Biden Emails," *Politico*, October 19, 2020, https://www.politico.com/f/?id=00000175-4393-d7aa-af77-579f 9b330000.

9 Glenn Kessler, "Dissecting GOP claims about Hunter Biden deals allegedly involving his father," *Washington Post*, November 23, 2022, https://www.washingtonpost.com/politics/2022/11/23/dissecting-gop -claims-about-hunter-biden-deals-allegedly-involving-his-father/.

10 Samuel Chamberlain, "Hunter Biden's ex-stripper baby mama was on his payroll while pregnant," *New York Post*, June 2, 2021, https:// nypost.com/2021/06/02/hunter-bidens-ex-stripper-baby-mama-was -on-his-payroll-while-pregnant-texts/.

11 "EXC: Hunter Biden's Texts Confirm Gun Was Taken, Left in Dumpster, 'Police, FBI, Secret Service Came on Scene,'" *National Pulse*, March 26, 2021, https://thenationalpulse.com/2021/03/26/exc -hunter-bidens-texts-confirm-gun-was-taken-left-in-dumpster-police -fbi-secret-service-came-on-scene/.

12 Kathleen Buhle, *If We Break: A Memoir of Marriage, Addiction, and Healing* (New York: Crown, 2022), 260.

13 Joseph A. Wulfsohn, "Twitter Files flashback: Jack Dorsey testified under oath Twitter does not censor, 'shadow-ban' conservatives," Fox News, December 9, 2022, https://www.foxnews.com/media/twitter -files-flashback-jack-dorsey-testified-oath-twitter-censor-shadow-ban -conservatives.

14 Brian Stelter, "Twitter's Jack Dorsey: 'We are not' discriminating against any political viewpoint," CNN, August 20, 2018, https:// money.cnn.com/2018/08/18/media/twitter-jack-dorsey-trump-social -media/index.html.

¹⁵ Michael Shellenberger tweet, December 10, 2022, https://
twittercom/ShellenbergerMD/status/1601720455005511680.

¹⁶ Jessica Chasmar, "James Baker, Twitter lawyer fired by Elon
Musk, played key role in FBI's Trump-Russia collusion probe,"
Fox News, December 7, 2022, https://www.foxnews.com/politics
/james-baker-twitter-lawyer-fired-elon-musk-played-key-role-fbi
-trump-russia-collusion-probe.

¹⁷ "San Diego Pastor Turns Church into Family-Friendly Strip Club
to Be Deemed 'Essential,'" WIBC, December 4, 2020, https://wibc
.com/99212/san-diego-pastor-turn-church-into-family-friendly-strip
-clubs-to-be-deemed-essential/.

¹⁸ Jerry Dunleavy, "Biden 'disinformation' chief a Trump dossier
fan and Hunter Biden laptop doubter," *Washington Examiner*, April
28, 2022, https://www.washingtonexaminer.com/news/bidens
-disinformation-chief-is-trump-dossier-author-fan-and-hunter
-laptop-doubter.

Count Three: The Trojan Horse

¹ "Fact check: 2006 video of Biden," Reuters, February 19, 2021,
https://www.reuters.com/article/uk-factcheck-biden-2006-video
/fact-check-2006-video-of-bidens-critical-mexico-remarks-was-not
-leaked-has-been-in-the-public-domain-and-reported-on-by-media
-outlets-idUSKBN2AJ2BF.

² Lindsay Kornick, "Karine Jean-Pierre faces backlash after claiming
the border is not open: 'A bold-faced lie,'" Fox News, December
20, 2022, https://www.foxnews.com/media/karine-jean-pierre-faces
-backlash-claiming-border-open-bold-faced-lie.

NOTES

3 "Nationwide Encounters," U.S. Customs and Border Protection, modified February 6, 2023, https://www.cbp.gov/newsroom/stats/nationwide-encounters.

4 Darragh Roche, "Disinformation Head Nina Jankowicz Addresses Hunter Biden Laptop Remarks," *Newsweek*, April 28, 2022, https://www.newsweek.com/disinformation-head-nina-jankowicz-hunter-biden-laptop-remarks-1701654.

5 Stephen M. Lepore, "Biden makes series of false claims as he addresses labor unions," *Daily Mail*, June 14, 2022, https://www.dailymail.co.uk/news/article-10917139/Biden-makes-series-false-claims-addresses-labor-unions-gets-angry-slams-lies.html.

6 Nicholas Vega, "American's now have an average of $9,000 les in savings than they did last year," CNBC, May 21, 2022, https://www.cnbc.com/2022/05/21/americans-now-have-an-average-of-9000-dollars-less-in-savings-than-in-2021.html#:~:text=The%20average%20amount%20of%20personal,highly%20disruptive%E2%80%9D%20to%20their%20finances.

7 Joe Perticone, "Flashback: Joe Biden's first presidential run in 1988 cratered amid multiple insances of plagiarism," Business Insider, March 12, 2019, https://www.businessinsider.com/plagiarism-scandal-joe-biden-first-presidential-run-1988-2019-3.

8 Allie Griffin, "Biden takes shot at Trump and Republicans on 'Jimmy Kimmel Live!'" *New York Post*, June 8, 2022, https://nypost.com/2022/06/08/biden-takes-shot-at-trump-and-republicans-on-jimmy-kimmel-live/.

9 Rachel Siegel, "June inflation soared 9.1%, a new 40-year high, amid spiking gas prices," *Washington Post*, July 13, 2022, https://www.washingtonpost.com/business/2022/07/13/inflation-june-cpi/.

[10] Zach Schonfeld, "88 percent say US is on wrong track: survey," *The Hill*, July 5, 2022, https://thehill.com/homenews/administration/3546548-88-percent-say-us-is-on-wrong-track-survey/.

[11] Adam Shaw, "Flashback: Kamala Harris Compared ICT to KKK in Senate Hearing," Fox News, August 11, 2020, https://www.foxnews.com/politics/kamala-harris-ice-kkk-senate-hearing.

[12] Robin Bravender, "Ex-Kamala Harris staffers have bad memories of a toxic culture in her past offices," *Insider*, July 14, 2021, https://www.businessinsider.com/kamala-harris-staffers-toxic-office-culture-dysfunction-2021-7.

Count Four: Pay to Play

[1] Tim Murphy, "House of Cards," *Mother Jones*, November/December 2019, https://www.motherjones.com/politics/2019/11/biden-bankruptcy-president/.

[2] Jim Geraghty, "Hunter Biden: The Most Comprehensive Timeline," *National Review*, September 30, 2019, https://www.nationalreview.com/2019/09/hunter-biden-comprehensive-timeline/.

[3] Geraghty, "Hunter Biden: The Most Comprehensive Timeline."

[4] As quoted in Andrew C. McCarthy, "Change (and a Few Dollars) You Can Believe In," *National Review*, August 28, 2008, https://www.nationalreview.com/corner/change-and-few-dollars-you-can-believe-andrew-c-mccarthy/.

[5] James V. Grimaldo and Kimberly Kindy, "Obama, Biden's Son Linked by Earmarks," *Washington Post*, August 27, 2008, https://www.washingtonpost.com/wp-dyn/content/article/2008/08/26/AR2008082603894.html.

6 Email to Devon Archer from Hunter Biden, March 4, 2013, https://bidenlaptopemails.com/biden-emails/email.php?id=20130304-223149_66841.

7 Peter Schweizer, *Secret Empires: How the American Political Class Hides Corruption and Enriches Family and Friends* (New York: HarperCollins, 2018), 29.

8 Adam Entous, "Will Hunter Biden Jeopardize His Father's Campaign?" *New Yorker*, July 1, 2019, https://www.newyorker.com/magazine/2019/07/08/will-hunter-biden-jeopardize-his-fathers-campaign.

9 Peter Schweizer, "The troubling reason why Biden is so soft on China," *New York Post*, May 11, 2019, "https://nypost.com/2019/05/11/the-troubling-reason-why-biden-is-so-soft-on-china/.

10 William H. McMichael and Jonathan Starkey, "Biden's son fails drug test, discharged from Navy," *USA Today*, October 17, 2014, https://www.usatoday.com/story/news/nation/2014/10/17/hunter-biden-drug-test/17427857/.

11 "Hunter Biden, Burisma, and Corruption: The Impact on U.S. Government Policy and Related Concerns," September 23, 2020, https://www.finance.senate.gov/imo/media/doc/HSGAC%20-%20Finance%20Joint%20Report%202020.09.23.pdf.

12 User Clip: "Biden Tells Story of Getting the Ukraine Prosecutor Fired," C-SPAN, January 23, 2018, https://www.c-span.org/video/?c4820105/user-clip-biden-tells-story-ukraine-prosecutor-fired.

13 Andrew Rice and Olivia Nuzzi, "The Sordid Saga of Hunter Biden's Laptop," *New York*, September 12, 2022, https://nymag.com/intelligencer/article/hunter-biden-laptop-investigation.html.

[14] Miranda Devine, "Joe Biden was involved in a deal with a Chinese giant," *New York Post*, November 29, 2021, https://nypost .com/2021/11/29/joe-biden-expected-10-percent-cut-in-deal-with -a-chinese-giant/.

[15] As quoted in Jim Geraghty, "The Remarkable Apathy about Biden-Family Corruption," *National Review*, August 19, 2022, https://www.nationalreview.com/the-morning-jolt/the-remarkable -apathy-about-biden-family-corruption/.

[16] Devine, "Joe Biden was involved in a deal with a Chinese giant," *New York Post.*

[17] Devine, "Joe Biden was involved."

[18] Devine, "Joe Biden was involved."

[19] Adam Entous, "Will Hunter Biden Jeopardize His Father's Campaign? *New Yorker*, July 1, 2019, https://www.newyorker.com /magazine/2019/07/08/will-hunter-biden-jeopardize-his-fathers -campaign.

[20] "Congress Approved $113 Billion of Aid in Ukraine in 2022," Committee for a Responsible Federal Budget, January 5, 2023, https://www.crfb.org/blogs/congress-approved-113-billion-aid -ukraine-2022.

[21] Nahal Toosi and Bryan Bender, "U.S. cable warns of major barriers to tracking Ukraine aid," *Politico*, December 14, 2022, https://www .politico.com/news/2022/12/14/us-ukraine-aid-cable-00073803.

Count Five: Crossing the Blue Line

[1] "How Informed Are Americans about Race and Policing?" Research Report: CUPES-007, February 20, 2021, https://www.skeptic.com /research-center/reports/Research-Report-CUPES-007.pdf.

[2] Statistics for 2019, https://www.washingtonpost.com/graphics/2019 /national/police-shootings-2019/.

[3] Statistics for 2021, https://www.washingtonpost.com/graphics /investigations/police-shootings-database/.

[4] Douglas Murray, *The War on the West* (New York: HarperCollins, 2022), 25.

[5] Zac Kriegman, "I Criticized BLM. Then I Was Fired," *The Free Press*, May 12, 2022, https://www.thefp.com/p/i-criticized-blm-then -i-was-fired.

[6] Kriegman, "I Criticized BLM."

[7] Mariame Kaba, "Yes, We Mean Literally Abolish the Police," *New York Times*, June 12, 2020, https://www.nytimes.com/2020/06/12 /opinion/sunday/floyd-abolish-defund-police.html.

[8] Martin Kaste, "Minneapolis voters reject a measure to replace city's police department," NPR, November 3, 2021, https://www.npr.org /2021/11/02/1051617581/minneapolis-police-vote.

[9] Jenny Gross and John Eligon, "Minneapolis City Council Votes to Remove $8 Million from Police Budget," *New York Times*, December 10, 2020, https://www.nytimes.com/2020/12/10/us/minneapolis -police-funding.html.

[10] AP, "Minneapolis Nears Record Homicide Count for 2021," *U.S. News & World Report*, December 31, 2021, https://www.usnews.com/news/best-states/minnesota/articles/2021-12-31/minneapolis-nears-record-homicide-count-for-2021.

[11] Paul Walsh, "Violent crime rose nearly 22% in Minnesota last year vs. 2020, state says," *StarTribune*, August 15, 2022, https://www.startribune.com/violent-crime-rose-21-in-minnesota-last-year-vs-2020-state-says/600198509/.

[12] Ibrahim Hirst, "Black Residents of Minneapolis Say They Need More Cops—Not Fewer," *The Nation*, September 30, 2021, https://www.thenation.com/article/politics/minneapolis-police-reform/.

[13] Hirst, "Black Residents."

[14] Jon Collins, "Poll: Public safety amendment has edge, but most want police cuts," MPR News. September 2021, https://www.mprnews.org/story/2021/09/18/poll-shows-support-for-public-safety-amendment-but-not-for-cutting-police-force.

[15] Collins, "Poll: Public safety amendment has edge, but most want police cuts."

[16] Alec Schemmel, "Mayor who pushed to defund police by $80M pleads with Feds to help with rampant crime," December 22, 2021, https://fox17.com/news/nation-world/mayor-who-pushed-to-defund-police-by-80m-pleads-with-feds-to-help-with-rampant-crime.

[17] "Portland Homicide Problem Analysis 2019–2021," https://www.portland.gov/sites/default/files/2022/2022-pdx-problem-analysis-public-version.pdf.

[18] Liz Burch, "'Another incredibly violent year': Portland's 2022 homicide number higher than 20-year average," KOIN, January 2,

2023, https://www.koin.com/news/crime/another-incredibly-violent
-year-portlands-2022-homicide-number-higher-than-20-year-average/.

[19] John Gramlich, "What we know about the increase in U.S. murders
in 2020," Pew Research Center, October 27, 2021, https://www
.pewresearch.org/fact-tank/2021/10/27/what-we-know-about-the
-increase-in-u-s-murders-in-2020/.

[20] Ben Leonard, "Biden draws bipartisan applause for calls to 'fund the
police,'" *Politico*, March 1, 2022, https://www.politico.com/news
/2022/03/01/state-of-the-union-2022-fund-police-00013065.

[21] James Gordon, "'Shut up b***h!' Toddler swings at Minnesota
cops," *Daily Mail*, July 12, 2022, https://www.dailymail.co.uk/news
/article-11004511/Shocking-moment-TODDLER-swings-cops
-Minnesota-officers-try-execute-warrant-murder-suspect.html.

[22] Andrew Kerr, "Major corporate donors silent on Black Lives
Matter's alleged self-dealing," *Washington Examiner*, June 3, 2022,
https://www.washingtonexaminer.com/news/major-corporate-donors
-silent-on-black-lives-matters-alleged-self-dealing.

[23] Isabel Vincent, "Inside BLM co-founder Patrisse Khan-Cullors'
million-dollar real estate buying binge," *New York Post*, April 10,
2021, https://nypost.com/2021/04/10/inside-blm-co-founder-patrisse
-khan-cullors-real-estate-buying-binge/.

[24] "One Year Later: Reflecting on 'Freedom Summer' and the
Anniversary of George Floyd | BLM Roundtable, YouTube, https://
www.youtube.com/watch?v=VYxH4m_S1HM.

[25] Sean Campbell, "Black Lives Matter Secretly Bought a $6 Million
House," *New York*, April 4, 2022, https://nymag.com/intelligencer
/2022/04/black-lives-matter-6-million-dollar-house.html.

26 Andrew Kerr, "BLM co-founder: Charity transparency laws are 'triggering,'" *Washington Examiner*, April 13, 2022, https://www .washingtonexaminer.com/news/blm-co-founder-charity-transparency -laws-are-triggering.

27 Snejana Farberov, "BLM co-founder Patrisse Cullors says her mistakes with 'white guilt money' were weaponized against her," *New York Post*, May 18, 2022, https://nypost.com/2022/05/18/ blm-co-founder-patrisse-cullors-says-white-guilt-money-mistakes -weaponized-against-her/.

Count Six: Aiding and Abetting Violent Criminal Conduct

1 Callie Patteson, "Psaki shrugs off crime concerns as part of 'alternate universe,'" *New York Post*, January 31, 2022 https://nypost .com/2022/01/31/psaki-shrugs-off-crime-fears-coverage-as-part -of-alternate-universe/.

2 Bernadette Hogan, Tina Moore, and Bruce Golding, "10 career criminals racked up nearly 500 arrests since NY bail reform began," *New York Post*, August 3, 2022, https://nypost.com/2022/08/03 /career-criminals-rack-up-nearly-500-arrests-since-ny-bail-reform -began/.

3 Kerry Burke and Elizabeth Keogh, "Man with 45 prior arrests nabbed for shoving stranger to Union Square subway tracks," *New York Daily News*, October 3, 2022, https://news.yahoo.com/man -shoved-tracks-union-square-024900160.html.

4 Carl Campanile, "AG Letitia James says 'spikes in crime' don't warrant changes to bail law," *New York Post*, May 11, 2022, https://

nypost.com/2022/05/11/ag-letitia-james-says-spikes-in-crime-dont -warrant-changes-to-bail/.

5 "129 officers killed in line of duty in 2021, FBI report says," Police1, June 14, 2022, https://www.police1.com/police-heroes/articles/129 -officers-killed-in-line-of-duty-in-2021-fbi-report-says-cFWzK En9J20qC0sH/.

6 Eric Shawn, "NY bail reform push faces blowback from crime victims in emotional protest," Fox News, February 7, 2022, https:// www.foxnews.com/us/new-york-bail-reform-push-crime-victims -protest.

7 Shawn, "NY bail reform push faces blowback."

8 Caroline Downey, "Biden: 'Negative Side of Bail Reform Is Vastly Overrated,'" National Review, May 13, 2022, https://www .nationalreview.com/news/biden-negative-side-of-bail-reform-is-vastly -overrated/.

9 Yaron Steinbuch, "DA blames assistant for Waukesha parade rampage suspect's 'inappropriately low' bail," New York Post, December 3, 2021, https://nypost.com/2021/12/03/da-blames-assistant-for -waukesha-rampage-suspects-inappropriately-low-bail/.

10 Scott Bland, "George Soros quiet overhaul of the U.S. justice system," Politico, August 30, 2016, https://www.politico.com/story /2016/08/george-soros-criminal-justice-reform-227519.

11 Jason Garcia, "Group with ties to billionaire George Soros spends $1.5 million lats-minute ads in Orange Osceola state attorney race," Orlando Sentinel, August 16, 2020, https://www.orlandosentinel.com /news/os-ne-monique-worrell-george-soros-state-attorney-20200816 -xgstfmgnlnbzrek5bbja4ykm6u-story.html.

12 "LELDF Original Research: Justice for Sale," June 2022, https://www.policedefense.org/leldf-justice-for-sale/.

13 Kyle Sammin, "What happens when a city's chief prosecutor refuses to prosecute?" *Philadelphia Inquirer*, June 17, 2022, https://www.inquirer.com/opinion/philadelphia-district-attorney-larry-krasner-impeachment-pennsylvania-legislature-20220617.html.

14 Parker Thayer, "Living Room Pundit's Guide to Soros District Attorneys," Capital Research Center, January 18, 2022, https://capitalresearch.org/article/living-room-pundits-guide-to-soros-district-attorneys/.

15 "Mapping Philadelphia's Gun Violence Crisis," https://controller.phila.gov/philadelphia-audits/mapping-gun-violence/#/?year=2016&layers=Point%20locations.

16 Joseph Vaughn, "Philly Cops Are Solving Fewer Homicides." The City Keeps Paying Them Millions," The Appeal, March 1, 2021, https://theappeal.org/philly-cops-are-solving-fewer-homicides-the-city-keeps-paying-them-millions/.

17 Chris Palmer, Ellie Rushing, and Anna Orso, "Philly DA Larry Krasner impeached by Pa. House, advancing GOP effort to remove him from office," *Philadelphia Inquirer*, November 16, 2022, https://www.inquirer.com/news/larry-krasner-impeachment-vote-pennsylvania-house-20221116.html.

18 James D. Schultz, "The Disastrous Consequences of DA Larry Krasner's 'Reforms,'" *Philadelphia*, June 27, 2019, https://www.phillymag.com/news/2019/06/27/larry-krasner-reforms-philadelphia/.

19 Chris Palmer, "Philly DA Larry Krasner is changing the way his office prosecutes killers. Not everyone agrees," *Philadelphia Inquirer*, April 4, 2018, https://www.inquirer.com/philly/news/crime/

philadelphia-district-attorney-larry-krasner-homicide-prosecutions
-lifers-anthony-voci.html.

20 Palmer, "Philly DA Larry Krasner."

21 Becky Willeke, "Three Missouri cities in top ten for most violent
crime rate in U.S." Fox 2Now, updated October 1, 2021, https://
fox2now.com/news/missouri/three-missouri-cities-in-top-ten-for
-most-violent-crime-rate-in-u-s/.

22 Zack Smith and Charles "Cully" Stimson, "Mett Kim Foxx, the
Rogue Prosecutor Whose Policies Are Wreaking Havoc in Chicago,"
The Heritage Foundation, November 3, 2020, https://www.heritage
.org/crime-and-justice/commentary/meet-kim-foxx-the-rogue
-prosecutor-whose-policies-are-wreaking-havoc.

23 https://www.kimfoxx.com/pledge

24 Leah Hope, "Report on Kim Foxx's office's handling of Jussie
Smollett case made public, judge rules," ABC7 Chicago, December
20, 2021, https://abc7chicago.com/jussie-smollett-kim-foxx-news
-sentence/11361612/.

25 Marjorie Hernandez and Emily Crane, "Special prosecutor report
found Kim Foxx's office mishandled Jussie Smollet case," *New York
Post*, December 20, 2021, https://nypost.com/2021/12/20/kim-foxxs
-office-failed-in-handling-jussie-smollett-case/.

26 Brittany Bernstein, "Manhattan DA Drops Murder Charge against
Bodega Worker Who Fatally Stabbed Attacker," *National Review*, July
19, 2022, https://www.nationalreview.com/news/manhattan-da-drops
-murder-charge-against-bodega-worker-who-fatally-stabbed-attacker/.

27 Yael Halon, "CNN roasted for tweet saying Waukesha parade
attack was caused by 'a car' that drove through parade," Fox News,

November 28, 2021, https://www.foxnews.com/media/waukesha -parade-attack-cnn-tweet-car-parade.

28 Chesa Boudin, "Across Prison Walls, I Felt My Parents' Love," *The Nation*, March 8, 2021, https://www.thenation.com/article/society /chesa-boudin-parents-prison/.

29 John Chisolm tweet, November 10, 2019, https://twitter.com /DAJohnChisholm/status/1193597241761681414.

30 Charles Stimson and Zack Smith, "George Gascón: A Rogue Prosecutor Whose Extreme Policies Undermine the Rule of Law and Make Los Angeles Less Safe," The Heritage Foundation, January 28, 2021, https://www.heritage.org/crime-and-justice/report/george -gascon-rogue-prosecutor-whose-extreme-policies-undermine-the-rule.

31 Audrey Conklin, "Gascon slammed for reversal on trans child molester Tubbs case: 'Utterly incompetent' or 'lying'?" Fox News, February 22, 2022, https://www.foxnews.com/us/gascon -slammed-reversal-child-molestor-hannah-tubbs-case.

32 Marjorie Hernandez and Emily Crane, "LA DA George Gascon's policies may cover funeral for cop-killer," *New York Post*, June 16, 2022, https://nypost.com/2022/06/16/la-da-george-gascons -policies-cover-funeral-for-cop-killer/.

Count Seven: The Infringement on the Right to Bear Arms

1 James Pollard and Patrick Svitek, "Beto O'Rourke went after assault rifles in his run for president. Will that hurt him with gun -loving Texans?" *Texas Tribune*, November 15, 2021, https://www .texastribune.org/2021/11/15/texas-beto-orourke-guns-2022/.

2 Katherine Schaeffer, "Key facts about Americans and guns," Pew Research Center, September 13, 2021, https://www.pewresearch.org /fact-tank/2021/09/13/key-facts-about-americans-and-guns/.

3 "Michael Bloomberg speaks in Aspen Colorado," February 5, 2015, https://www.youtube.com/watch?v=1bbjB3jVGRU.

4 John Gramlich, "What the data says about gun deaths in the U.S." Pew Research Center, February 3, 2022, https://www.pewresearch .org/fact-tank/2022/02/03/what-the-data-says-about-gun-deaths-in -the-u-s/.

5 Ben Smith, "Obama on small-town Pa.: Clinging to guns, religion, xenophobia," *Politico*, April 11, 2008, https://www.politico.com /blogs/ben-smith/2008/04/obama-on-small-town-pa-clinging-to -religion-guns-xenophobia-007737.

6 Lawrence Richard, "Philadelphia shooting: Dem mayor rips Second Amendment, says only the police should have guns," Fox News, July 5, 2022, https://www.foxnews.com/us/philly-mayor-second -amendment-officers-shot-july-fourth.

7 Lawrence Richard, "Philadelphia shooting: Dem mayor rips Second Amendment, says only the police should have guns," Fox News, July 5, 2022, https://www.foxnews.com/us/philly-mayor-second -amendment-officers-shot-july-fourth.

8 "Mapping Philadelphia's Gun Violence Crisis," https://controller .phila.gov/philadelphia-audits/mapping-gun-violence/#/?year=2021 &layers=Point%20locations&map=11.00%2F39.98500%2F-75 .15000.

9 Mariel Alper and Lauren Glaze, "Source and Use of Firearms Involved in Crimes, Survey of Prison Inmates, 2016," U.S.

Department of Justice Special Report, January 2019, https://bjs.ojp
.gov/content/pub/pdf/suficspi16.pdf.

[10] "Iron Pipeline: 14 charged for allegedly trafficking nearly 400 guns
to the Philadelphia area from south," Fox 29, April 11, 2022, https://
www.fox29.com/news/officials-announce-charges-in-connection-with
-illegal-trafficking-of-nearly-400-guns-to-the-philadelphia-area.

[11] Mélissa Godin, "What the U.S. Can Learn from Countries
Where Cops Don't Carry Guns," *Time*, June 19, 2020, https://time
.com/5854986/police-reform-defund-unarmed-guns/.

[12] Morgan Gstalter, "Minneapolis City Council members get private
security detail after reported threats," The Hill, June 27, 2020, https://
thehill.com/homenews/state-watch/504831-minneapolis-city-council
-members-get-private-security-detail-after/.

[13] Erik Runge, "'I'm out in the public eye': Mayor Lightfoot gets aircut
amid social distancing orders," WGN9, April 6, 2020, https://wgntv
.com/news/coronavirus/im-out-in-the-public-eye-mayor-lightfoot
-gets-haircut-amid-social-distancing-orders/https://wgntv.com/news
/coronavirus/im-out-in-the-public-eye-mayor-lightfoot-gets-haircut
-amid-social-distancing-orders/.

[14] Existential Comics tweet, May 27, 2020, https://twitter.com
/existentialcoms/status/1265723520916414464.

[15] Jon Jackson, "Biden on Second Amendment: When It Was Passed,
'You Couldn't Buy a Cannon,'" *Newsweek*, May 30, 2022, https://
www.newsweek.com/biden-second-amendment-when-passed-couldnt
-buy-cannon-1711480.

[16] Glenn Kessler, "Biden's false claim that the 2nd Amendment
bans cannon ownership," *Washington Post*, June 28, 2021,

https://www.washingtonpost.com/politics/2021/06/28/bidens-false-claim-that-2nd-amendment-bans-cannon-ownership/.

[17] Guest Essay, "A Supreme Court Head-Scratcher: Is a Colonial Musket 'Analogous' to an AR-15?'" *New York Times*, July 1, 2022, https://www.nytimes.com/2022/07/01/opinion/guns-supreme-court.html.

[18] "Second Amendment," Constitution of the United States, https://constitution.congress.gov/constitution/amendment-2/.

[19] Antonin Scalia, *The Essential Scalia: On the Constitution, the Courts, and the Rule of Law* (New York: Crown Forum, 2020), 21.

[20] *District of Columbia v. Heller*, June 26, 2008, https://www.law.cornell.edu/supct/html/07-290.ZO.html.

[21] Andrew Rosenthal, "Justice Scalia's Gun-Control Argument," *New York Times*, December 11, 2015, https://archive.nytimes.com/takingnote.blogs.nytimes.com/2015/12/11/justice-scalias-gun-control-argument/.

[22] Jason J. Brown, "Deconstructing the Anti-Gun Second Amendment 'Musket Myth,'" NRA Blog, October 13, 2016, https://www.nrablog.com/articles/2016/10/deconstructing-the-anti-gun-second-amendment-musket-myth/.

[23] John Paul Stevens, "Repeal the Second Amendment," *New York Times*, March 27, 2018, https://www.nytimes.com/2018/03/27/opinion/john-paul-stevens-repeal-second-amendment.html.

[24] Peter Suciu, "Why Gun Sales Are Going Back Up (Again)," *19FortyFive*, July 2022, https://www.19fortyfive.com/2022/07/why-gun-sales-are-going-back-up-again/.

[25] Maureen Dowd, "Eric Adams, the Mayor Who Never Sleeps," *New York Times*, July 8, 2022, https://www.nytimes.com/2022/07/08 /opinion/eric-adams-mayor-new-york.html?partner=IFTTT.

[26] Zachary Faria, "Kathy Hochul says she doesn't need proof that gun control keeps anyone safe," *Washington Examiner*, June 30, 2022, https://www.washingtonexaminer.com/opinion/kathy-hochul-says -she-doesnt-need-proof-that-gun-control-keeps-anyone-safe.

[27] Matthew Miller, Wilson Zhang, Deborah Azrael, "Firearm Purchasing During the COVID-19 Pandemic https://pubmed.ncbi .nlm.nih.gov/34928699/.

Count Eight: Illegal Crossings

[1] Joe Biden, "My Plan to Safely Reopen America," *New York Times*, April 12, 2020, https://www.nytimes.com/2020/04/12/opinion/joe -biden-coronavirus-reopen-america.html.

[2] "The Biden Plan for an Effective Re-Opening that Jumpstarts the Economy," https://joebiden.com/reopening/.

[3] "The Biden Plan for Securing Our Values as a Nation of Immigrants," https://joebiden.com/immigration/.

[4] "The Biden Plan for Securing Our Values as a Nation of Immigrants."

[5] "Executive Order on Restoring Faith in Our Legal Immigration Systems and Strengthening Integration and Inclusion Efforts for New Americans," The White House, February 2, 2021, https://www .whitehouse.gov/briefing-room/presidential-actions/2021/02/02/ executive-order-restoring-faith-in-our-legal-immigration-systems-and -strengthening-integration-and-inclusion-efforts-for-new-americans/.

6 "Remarks by President Biden at Signing of Executive Orders Advancing His Priority to Modernize Our Immigration System," The White House, February 2, 2021, https://www.whitehouse.gov /briefing-room/speeches-remarks/2021/02/02/remarks-by-president -biden-at-signing-of-executive-orders-advancing-his-priority-to -modernize-our-immigration-system/.

7 All 2020–22 statistics on the Southwest Land Border are from U.S. Customs and Border Protections, https://www.cbp.gov/newsroom /stats/southwest-land-border-encounters.

8 Jeff Mason, "Biden administration will appeal lifting mask mandate, if CDC agrees," Reuters, April 20, 2022, https://www.reuters.com /world/us/biden-administration-may-appeal-ruling-mask-mandates -white-house-says-2022-04-19/.

9 Stef W. Kight, "Scoop: 50,000 migrants released; few report to ICE," Axios, July 27, 2021, https://www.axios.com/2021/07/27 /migrant-release-no-court-date-ice-dhs-immigration.

10 Priscilla Alvarez, "Biden administrations announces official end to Title 42, the Trump-era pandemic restrictions at the US border," CNN, April 1, 2022, https://www.cnn.com/2022/04/01/politics /immigration-title-42-repeal-cdc/index.html.

11 Nick Miroff, "Biden official: Title 42 end will lead to fewer border crossings," *Washington Post*, May 5, 2022, https://www .washingtonpost.com/national-security/2022/05/05/border-title42 -biden/.

12 Miranda Devine et al., "Biden secretly flying underage migrants into NY in dead of night," *New York Post*, October 18, 2021, https://nypost.com/2021/10/18/biden-secretly-flying-underage -migrants-into-ny-in-dead-of-night/.

[13] Devine et al., "Biden secretly flying underage migrants."

[14] Matthew Watkins, "Second bus with migrants arrives outside Kamala Harris' residence," *Texas Tribune*, September 17, 2022, https://www.texastribune.org/2022/09/17/greg-abbott-migrant-busing/.

[15] Kerry J. Byrne, "Martha's Vineyard residents lament lack of resources, even as island is flush with cash and beds," Fox News, September 18, 2022, https://www.foxnews.com/lifestyle/marthas-vineyard-residents-lament-lack-resources-island-flush-cash-beds.

[16] "Annual Regional Overview," Missing Migrants Project, January–December 2021, https://missingmigrants.iom.int/sites/g/files/tmzbdl601/files/publication/file/MMP%20annual%20regional%20overview%202021%20LAC_Executive%20Summary-ENG_0.pdf.

[17] Rich Connell and Robert J. Lopez, "An Inside Look at 18th St.'s Menace," *Los Angeles Times*, November 17, 1996, https://www.latimes.com/archives/la-xpm-1996-11-17-mn-1539-story.html.

[18] "Border Patrol Agents Arrest Criminal Sex Offenders and Gang Members in RGV," Shore News Network, April 21, 2022, https://www.shorenewsnetwork.com/2022/04/21/border-patrol-agents-arrest-criminal-sex-offenders-and-gang-members-in-rgv/.

[19] "RGV Agents Apprehend Criminal Migrants and Gang Members," Shore News Network, May 22, 2022, https://www.shorenewsnetwork.com/2022/05/22/rgv-agents-apprehend-criminal-migrants-and-gang-members/.

[20] Anders Hagstrom, "Terror watchlist arrests have exploded at the border under Biden," Fox News, January 22, 2023, https://www.foxnews.com/politics/terror-watch-lists-arrests-exploded-border-biden.

21 Charles Payne, "'Your World,' on Title 42 Rollback, Ukraine-Russia War," Fox News, April 20, 2022, https://www.foxnews.com/transcript /your-world-on-title-42-rollback-ukraine-russia-war.

22 Shannon Pettypiece, "Biden says officials seen chasing Haitian on horseback 'will pay,'" NBC News, September 24, 2021, https://www .nbcnews.com/politics/white-house/biden-says-officials-seen-chasing -haitians-horseback-will-pay-n1280032.

23 Darragh Roche, "Video of Kamala Harris Blasting Border Treatment of Migrants Viewed Over 1M Times," *Newsweek*, September 22, 2021, https://www.newsweek.com/video-kamala-harris-blasting-border -treatment-migrants-viewed-over-1m-times-1631411.

24 Mike Berg tweet, September 22, 2021, https://twitter.com/MikeK Berg/status/1440759107770728457.

25 Bradford Betz, "Mayorkas testifies DHS is creating 'Disinformation Governance Board,'" Fox News, April 27, 2022, https://www.foxnews .com/politics/mayorkas-dhs-disinformation-governance-board.

26 Tom Homan, "Biden Owes Border Patrol Belated Apology Over Phony Charges of 'Whipping Illegal Aliens,'" The Heritage Foundation, March 25, 2022, https://www.heritage.org/progressivism /commentary/biden-owes-border-patrol-belated-apology-over-phony -charges-whipping.

27 MaryAnn Martinez, "Three Border Patrol agents die by suicide in three weeks," *New York Post*, November 30, 2022, https://nypost .com/2022/11/30/three-border-patrol-agents-die-by-suicide-in -three-weeks/.

28 Daniella Diaz, Betsy Klein, and Brenda Goodman, "Breaking down the Biden administration's response to the baby formula shortage,"

CNN, June 3, 2022, https://www.cnn.com/2022/06/03/politics/baby
-formula-crisis-timeline/index.html.

Count Nine: The Marxist Aversion of Democracy

[1] "The Life of Julia," https://www.youtube.com/watch?v=oqBjX
P8RKho.

[2] James Taranto, "The Lonely Life of Julia," *Wall Street Journal*, May 3,
2012, https://www.wsj.com/articles/SB100014240527023047437045
77382170789179442.

[3] Abigail Adams, "President Joe Biden and Dr. Jill Biden Honor
2022 Teacher of the Year in White House Ceremony," *People*, April
28, 2022, https://people.com/politics/president-joe-biden-and-dr-jill
-biden-honor-2022-teacher-of-the-year-in-white-house-ceremony/.

[4] Sam P. K. Collins, "Kurt Russell, National Teacher of the Year,
Stands Firm on Equity, Representation," *Washington Informer*, May
25, 2022, https://www.washingtoninformer.com/kurt-russell-national
-teacher-of-the-year-stands-firm-on-equity-representation/.

[5] Adams, "President Joe Biden and Dr. Jill Biden Honor 2022 Teacher
of the Year."

[6] Alec Schemmel, "'They're all our children': Biden emboldens
teachers amid debate about parental rights," KATV, April 28, 2022,
https://katv.com/news/nation-world/theyre-all-our-children-biden
-emboldens-teachers-amid-debate-about-parental-rights.

[7] "The Principles of Communism," (1847), https://www.marxists.org
/archive/marx/works/1847/11/prin-com.htm.

8 "The Communist Manifesto" by Karl Marx and Friedrich Engels, https://www.gutenberg.org/files/61/61-h/61-h.htm.

9 Paul Kengor, "Americans Buy into Marxist Family Planning," *The Federalist*, June 29, 2015, https://thefederalist.com/2015/06/29/americans-buy-into-marxist-family-planning/.

10 Mike Gonzalez, "Socialism and Family," The Heritage Foundation, March 1, 2022, https://www.heritage.org/marriage-and-family/commentary/socialism-and-family.

11 Michelle Ye Hee Lee, "Frank Marshall Davis: Obama's 'Communist mentor'?" *Washington Post*, March 23, 2015, https://www.washingtonpost.com/news/fact-checker/wp/2015/03/23/frank-marshall-davis-obamas-communist-mentor/.

12 Paul Kengor, *The Communist: Frank Marshall Davis: The Untold Story of Barack Obama's Mentor* (New York: Threshold Editions, 2012), 15.

13 Barack Obama, *A Promised Land* (New York: Crown Publishing, 2020), 10.

14 "Fact Sheet: The American Family Plan," The White House, April 28, 2021, https://www.whitehouse.gov/briefing-room/statements-releases/2021/04/28/fact-sheet-the-american-families-plan/.

15 "Fact Sheet: The American Family Plan."

16 Christopher F. Rufo, "Failure Factory," *City Journal*, February 23, 2021, https://www.city-journal.org/buffalo-public-schools-critical-race-theory-curriculum.

17 Rufo, "Failure Factory."

18 Rufo, "Failure Factory."

[19] Rufo, "Failure Factory."

[20] Bettina Love, as quoted by Christopher F. Rufo, "Teaching Hate," *City Journal*, December 18, 2020, https://www.city-journal.org/racial -equity-programs-seattle-schools.

[21] Christopher F. Rufo, "Woke Elementary," *City Journal*, January 13, 2021, https://www.city-journal.org/identity-politics-in-cupertino -california-elementary-school.

[22] Tucker Carlson, "Democrats and the media are lying about Florida's Parental Rights in Education bill," Fox News, March 29, 2022, https://www.foxnews.com/opinion/tucker-carlson-democrats-media -lying-florida-parental-rights-education-bill.

[23] "Terry McAuliffe's War on Parents," *National Review*, October 1, 2021, https://www.nationalreview.com/2021/10/terry-mcauliffes-war -on-parents/.

[24] Luke Rosiak, "Loudoun County Schools Tried to Conceal Sexual Assault Against Daughter in Bathroom, Father Says," *Daily Wire*, 2022, https://www.dailywire.com/news/loudoun-county-schools-tried -to-conceal-sexual-assault-against-daughter-in-bathroom-father-says.

[25] "Full NSBA Letter to Biden Administration and Department of Justice Memo," Parents Defending Education, November 29, 2021, https://defendinged.org/press-releases/full-nsba-letter-to-biden -administration-and-department-of-justice-memo/.

[26] "Garland says authorities will target school board threats," *The Ledger*, October 1, 2021, http://www.tnledger.com/editorial/article .aspx?id=146298.

[27] Timothy H. J. Nerozzi, "Randi Weingarten says parental rights bills are 'the way in which wars start,'" Fox News, April 22, 2022,

https://www.foxnews.com/us/randi-weingarten-parental-rights
-bills-the-way-in-which-wars-start.

[28] Lindsay Kornick, "MSNBC's Nicolle Wallace compares DeSantis, Youngkin education bills to Russian soldiers raping children," Fox News, April 20, 2022, https://www.foxnews.com/media/msnbc -nicolle-wallace-desantis-youngkin-education-bills.

Count Ten: Gaslighting

[1] BBVA statement of purpose on website, accessed February 18, 2023, https://www.bbva.com/en/whats-happening-davos-forum/.

[2] "'Our house is on fire': Greta Thunberg, 16, urges leaders to act on climate," *The Guardian*, January 25, 2019, https://www. theguardian.com/environment/2019/jan/25/our-house-is-on-fire -greta-thunberg16-urges-leaders-to-act-on-climate.

[3] John Bowden, "Ocasio-Cortez: 'World will end in 12 years' if climate change not addressed," *The Hill*, January 22, 2019, https:// thehill.com/policy/energy-environment/426353-ocasio-cortez-the -world-will-end-in-12-years-if-we-dont-address/.

[4] "'Our house is on fire': Greta Thunberg.

[5] Paul Bois, "Comedian Konstantin Kisin Obliterates Woke Culture in Viral Oxford University Debate," Breitbart, January 16, 2023, https:// www.breitbart.com/politics/2023/01/16/watch-comedian-konstantin -kisin-obliterates-woke-culture-in-viral-oxford-union-debate/.

[6] Michael Shellenberger, "The Reason Renewables Can't Power Modern Civilization Is Because They Were Never Meant To," *Forbes*, May 6, 2019, https://www.forbes.com/sites/michael shellenberger/2019/05/06/the-reason-renewables-cant-power

-modern-civilization-is-because-they-were-never-meant-to/?sh
=4ba60f1eea2b.

[7] David McHugh, Colleen Barry, Joe McDonald, and Tatiana Pollastri, "Energy crunch hits global recovery as winter approaches," AP News, October 19, 2021, https://apnews.com/article/coronavirus-pandemic -lifestyle-business-russia-health-70b97e36da53f62eba588b44f2b39 4bc.

[8] Thomas Barrabi, "Biden waiving Nord Stream 2 pipeline sanctions puts US at 'competitive disadvantage': GOP leader McCarthy," Fox News, June 9, 2021, https://www.foxnews.com/politics/biden -waiving-nord-stream-2-pipeline-sanctions-mccarthy.

[9] Lauren Sommer, "California Governor Signs Order Banning Sales of New Gasoline Cars by 2035," NPR, September 23, 2020, https:// www.npr.org/2020/09/23/916209659/california-governor-signs -order-banning-sales-of-new-gasoline-cars-by-2035.

[10] "California Releases Report Charting Path to 100 Percent Clean Electricity," California Energy Commission, March 15, 2021, https://www.energy.ca.gov/news/2021-03/california-releases -report-charting-path-100-percent-clean-electricity.

[11] "What Makes Natural Gas the Cleanest Fossil Fuel?" Accessed February 18, 2023, https://www.igs.com/energy-resource-center /energy-101/what-makes-natural-gas-the-cleanest-fossil-fuel#:~:text =Natural%20Gas%20is%20More%20Efficient,only%20a%20 32%25%20efficiency%20rate.

[12] Stephen M. Lepor, "Biden agrees to pay climate reparations," *Daily Mail*, November 19, 2022, https://www.dailymail.co.uk/news /article-11448109/Biden-agrees-pay-climate-reparations-compensate -developing-countries-global-warming.html.

[13] Valerie Volcovici, "Exclusive: Presidential hopeful Biden looks for 'middle ground' climate policy," *Reuters*, May 10, 2019, https://www.reuters.com/article/uk-usa-election-biden-climate-exclusive-idUKKCN1SG18C.

[14] William Cummings, "Tell her to 'look at my record': Biden responds to Ocasio-Cortez's criticism on climate," *USA Today*, Mary 14, 2019, https://www.usatoday.com/story/news/politics/onpolitics/2019/05/14/joe-biden-answers-alexandria-ocasio-cortez-climate-change-criticism/3665930002/.

[15] "The Biden Plan for a Clean Energy Revolution and Environmental Justice," https://joebiden.com/climate-plan/.

[16] Maureen Dowd, "Biden's Debate Finale: An Echo from Abroad," *New York Times*, September 12, 1987, https://www.nytimes.com/1987/09/12/us/biden-s-debate-finale-an-echo-from-abroad.html.

[17] Biden: "I Guarantee You We're Going to End Fossil Fuels," https://www.youtube.com/watch?v=OJ7MMsheHzQ.

[18] Sara Cook, Weijia Jiang, Matthew Mosk, "Biden administration cancels Alaska oil and gas lease sale," *CBS News*, May 18, 2022, https://www.cbsnews.com/news/biden-alaska-oil-gas-lease-sale-canceled/.

[19] Jason Plautz, "The Environmental Burden of Generation Z," *Washington Post*, February 3, 2020, https://www.washingtonpost.com/magazine/2020/02/03/eco-anxiety-is-overwhelming-kids-wheres-line-between-education-alarmism/.

[20] Callie Patteson, "Biden praises high gas prices as part of 'incredible transition,'" *New York Post*, May 23, 2022, https://nypost.com/2022/05/23/biden-praises-gas-prices-as-part-of-incredible-transition/.

Count Eleven: The Misinformation Game

[1] Jennifer Rubin, "Obama's speech at the United Nations," *Washington Post*, September 25, 2012, https://www.washingtonpost.com/blogs/right-turn/post/obamas-speech-at-the-united-nations/2012/09/25/4f207d8c-0728-11e2-a10c-fa5a255a9258_blog.html.

[2] *Brandenburg v. Ohio*, 395 U.S. 444 (1969), https://supreme.justia.com/cases/federal/us/395/444/.

[3] Karine Jean-Pierre tweet, December 17, 2016, https://twitter.com/K_JeanPierre/status/810294911815847936.

[4] President Clinton speaks in Chicago regarding election, Palmer House Hilton Hotel, January 9, 2001, https://grabien.com/getmedia.php?id=1571945&key=c85b8617c932d7ed8788fee715273f72&userid=17087.

[5] Ian Hanchett, "Wasserman Schultz: Al Gore Won Florida in 2000, 'The Supreme Court Elected the President,'" Breitbart, September 16, 2016, https://www.breitbart.com/clips/2016/09/16/wasserman-schultz-al-gore-won-florida-in-2000-the-supreme-court-elected-the-president/.

[6] "2008: Barack Obama Discusses Election Fraud," https://www.youtube.com/watch?v=3Gb3jzzn3hU.

[7] Bill Chappell, "Jimmy Carter Says He Sees Trump as an Illegitimate President," NPR, June 28, 2019, https://www.npr.org/2019/06/28/737008785/jimmy-carter-says-he-sees-trump-as-an-illegitimate-president.

[8] "President Jimmy Carter: Bush Didn't Win in 2000," https://www.youtube.com/watch?v=roTd_X6rQ34.

[9] Karine Jean-Pierre tweet, April 2, 2020, https://twitter.com/K_ JeanPierre/status/1245752237353308160.

[10] Rebecca Falconer, "Biden slams MAGA Republicans for 'semi-fascism,'" Axios, August 25, 2022, https://www.axios .com/2022/08/26/biden-maga-republicans-semi-fascism-maryland -rally.

[11] "Biden's latest, lowest drive to divide America," *New York Post*, August 31, 2022, https://nypost.com/2022/08/31/bidens-latest -lowest-drive-to-divide-america/.

[12] Jim Geraghty, "Blood-Red Dark Biden," *National Review*, September 2, 2022, https://www.nationalreview.com/the-morning -jolt/blood-red-dark-biden/.

[13] "On This Day: The first bitter, contested presidential election takes place," National Constitution Center, November 4, 2022, https://constitutioncenter.org/blog/on-this-day-the-first-bitter -contested-presidential-election-takes-place.

[14] "Southern congressman beats Northern senator with a cane in the halls of Congress," May 22, 1856, https://www.history.com /this-day-in-history/southern-congressman-attacks-northern-senator.

[15] Ben Smith, "Obama on small-town Pa.: Clinging to guns, religion, xenophobia," *Politico*, April 11, 2008, https://www.politico.com /blogs/ben-smith/2008/04/obama-on-small-town-pa-clinging-to -religion-guns-xenophobia-007737.

[16] Katie Reilly, "Read Hillary Clinton's 'Basket of Deplorables' Remark about Donald Trump Supporters," *Time*, September 10, 2016, https:// time.com/4486502/hillary-clinton-basket-of-deplorables-transcript/.

[17] Charles Creitz, "Nicholas Sandmann reaches settlement with NBC in Covington Catholic High School controversy," *New York Post*, December 18, 2021, https://nypost.com/2021/12/18/covington-catholic-graduate-nicholas-sandmann-settlement-with-nbc/.

[18] Emily Ekins, "51% of Strong Liberals Say It's Morally Acceptable to Punch Nazis," CATO Institute, November 3, 2017, https://www.cato.org/blog/51-strong-liberals-say-its-morally-acceptable-punch-nazis.

[19] Tyler Olson, "Biden again attacks 'MAGA' GOP members of Congress, 'full of anger, violence and hate,' in Labor Day speech," Fox News, September 5, 2022, https://www.foxnews.com/politics/biden-attacks-maga-gop-members-congress-full-anger-violence-hate-labor-day-speech.

[20] Rachael Bunyan, "'The country is no longer a democracy': Wanda Sykes," *Daily Mail*, June 29, 2022, https://www.dailymail.co.uk/news/article-10964331/The-country-no-longer-democracy-Wanda-Sykes-lays-Scotus-judges-lied.html.

[21] Maria Jimenez Moy et al., "Biden Calls State Decisions to End Mask Mandates 'Neanderthal Thinking,'" *New York Times*, updated March 10, 2021, https://www.nytimes.com/2021/03/03/us/texas-abbott-masks-coronavirus.html.